Violence and Compassion in the Novels of
WILLIAM STYRON
A Study in Tragic Humanism

VIOLENCE AND COMPASSION IN THE NOVELS OF WILLIAM STYRON

A Study in Tragic Humanism

S. LAXMANA MURTHY
Professor, Department of English
Kakatiya University

PRESTIGE

PRESTIGE BOOKS
NEW DELHI

ISBN 81-85218-03-X

First Published: 1988

Published by:
Prestige Books
3/28, East Patel Nagar
New Delhi 110 008
Phone: 5710787

Printed by:
Creative Printers
at Pal Mohan Process
W.Z. 130-A, Naraina
New Delhi 110 028

CONTENTS

Dedicated

to

PROFESSOR K. VENKATA RAMIAH
Member, Union Public Service Commission

with

love and gratitude

PREFACE

Since the publication of his first novel *Lie Down in Darkness* (1951) the critical scholarship of Styron has increased impressively. He has established himself as a major contemporary writer with his subsequent novels: *The Long March* (1952), *Set This House on Fire* (1960) and *The Confessions of Nat Turner* (1967). He has inspired, over years, a sustained critical debate based on incisive analyses of his fiction. Much of the critical writing on Styron, however, has interpreted him in the context of the Southern mode. Though a few recurrent regionalistic themes in his novels, to be sure, have given scope and credence to this kind of critical concern, Styron is not too happy with such a constrictive approach to his fiction. He has gone on record to say that it is his business to create characters that would be meaningful and relevant outside the Southern context as well. The other major critical stance in regard to Styron has been, in the main, concerned with the impact of Faulkner's pattern on the young writer. Styron has acknowledged the fact that though the influence of Faulkner was the hardest for him to shake off, he only accepted Faulkner's "complexity" without his "confusion." In addition, quite a few articles in several scholarly journals have been content to analyse the novelist's stylistic and sociological predilections—the latter particularly after the publication of *The Confessions of Nat Turner*. Criticism has not given, in my opinion, adequate attention to Styron's evolving awareness of modern human condition shaping his fiction. Hence there is a need to study Styron's thematic concerns especially in the context of man's complex predicament today marked by global violence and degeneration of human values. The search for values has also been the central theme of Albert Camus' work. Styron has admitted the influence of Camus in his intellectual make-up. Camus' tragic humanism therefore provides helpful insights in the study of Styron who has always insisted on staying human in a world imperilled by violence in various forms. He brings into focus through his novels the tragic fact of human existence and a constant endeavour to affirm love and compassion despite the nihilistic terror caused by ubiquitous violence in the modern world.

The present study is an attempt to analyse Styron's four novels *Lie Down in Darkness, The Long March, Set This House on Fire* and *The Confessions of Nat Turner* to explore his increasing consciousness of violence and compassion as constants of tragic human existence—from the stage of muted suggestion of the power of compassion in *Lie Down in Darkness* to its unequivocal affirmation in *The Confessions of Nat Turner.*

In preparing this project, I have benefited by the invaluable insights of numerous Styron scholars. I have acknowledged the fact at appropriate places in the study. In this context, I would particularly like to mention the valuations of Louis D. Rubin, Jr., Marc L. Ratner, Robert H. Fossum and Richard Pearce.

S. Laxmana Murthy

ACKNOWLEDGEMENTS

I wish to record my deep debt of gratitude to my teacher Dr. Satyanarain Singh, Professor of English, Osmania University, Hyderabad who has kindly guided my research with scholarly advice, meticulous care and personal affection.

I am grateful to Professor K. Venkata Ramiah, former Vice-Chancellor, Kakatiya University who has been an unfailing source of inspiration to me. My debt in so many ways to him cannot be expressed adequately.

I am thankful to the Director of American Studies Research Centre for permitting me to spend several weeks at Centre's library collecting material for my research.

I thank the University Grants Commission for providing me partial financial assistance for the publication of doctoral dissertation. I am thankful to Prof. T. Vasudev, Vice-Chancellor and Prof. Dinker Sirdeshmukh, Coordinating Officer (UGC Unit) of Kakatiya University who have helped me greatly in this regard.

I am highly obliged to Dr. R.K. Dhawan of Delhi University for his unstinted help and advice. My thanks are due to my friend Dr. M. Rajagopalachari who has prepared the press copy.

I am thankful to M/s Prestige Books who have brought out the book neatly and promptly.

S. LAXMANA MURTHY

1

Styron's Tragic Humanism: The Contexts of Violence and Compassion

Since the publication of his first novel *Lie Down in Darkness* (1951) Styron has largely been interpreted in terms of his Southern background. His subsequent novels, however, have made it look simplistic to explain away their thematic complexity as a regionalistic mode. Grappling with the fundamentals of human existence Styron's novels have compelled revolution in the context of his Christian and existential predilections and in the wider perspective of European tradition. It must, however, be remarked that Styron has never totally repudiated his Southern background. He recognises that the sources of his native literary tradition have been integral to his work. His ambiguity in relation to the South is only a pointer to the fact that his awareness of human predicament cannot be explicated in full by isolating and enlarging a few of the elements evident in his work: the Southern, the Christian and the existential. A proper appreciation of Styron could be possible by evaluating his tragic vision of man as born of the integral impact of these various elements. His grasp of human predicament as tragic is qualified by the fact that he is a modern Southern writer of the post-war generation sensitively alive to the major fictional concerns of Europe especially France. It is, therefore, necessary to relate Styron's Southernness to the contemporary tragic humanistic thought in the dialectical context of violence and compassion.

II

Though born and raised in Newport News, Virginia, Styron's allegiance to the Southern school has never been unqualified. Nevertheless, he admits that "the South has a definite literary tradition."[1] The Southern literature is believed to function within the confines of a particular cultural setting and lends itself to "meaningful elaborations upon its intrinsic nature."[2] "The Southern Temper" is defined as the concurrence of a sense of the concrete, the elemental, the ornamental and the representative giving it a sense of totality. In the view of Robert Heilman the Southern temper becomes "a condition of major art and mature thought."[3]

Louis D. Rubin holds that from Ellen Glasgow to William Styron, the writers of the twentieth century South have shared the milieu with their fellow Southerners. He believes that the social framework of the South participates in their writing organically in contrast to any other mode of fiction.[4] A sense of place, therefore, becomes significant in the thematic pattern of a defined body of literature like the modern Southern writing.

Further, the writers of the Southern school have adopted the Biblical rhetoric in style and a deep religious concern in theme. In addition, the social framework impinges on the individual so fully that he ceases to exist meaningfully outside of it. They view the individual as a product of historicity, elaborating the individual's commitment to society and his determining role within it.

The novels of William Styron, James Agee, George Garrett and Flannery O'Connor have provided a sharp contrast to the earlier Southern fiction like that of Faulkner which functioned predominantly with "a sense of intense involvement in a fixed, defined society,"[5] and which viewed life as meaningful in its identification with a place. The younger Southern writers have realised the need to get free from the rigid and restrictive reliance upon the traditional Southern modes. They give evidence of their being "Southern" by their conception of man as limited and dependent, and also by their rhetoric. They attempt to disengage themselves from the past as the haunting sceptre. The protagonists of their fiction confront and live "in a fluid changing world."[6]

There are, in fact, certain important features of the Southern school which define its identity: the role of the Negro, the awareness of man's limitations along with the almost religious recognition of infinite and unknowable powers, a probe into the values of society and the function of individual within the societal framework, the primitive celebration of land and its people and finally the conflict between the intellect and emotion. Added to this cluster is the disposition in a great measure to employ symbol and allegory as stylistic strategies.

Styron shares these many ideas with his compatriots, and yet his participation in the Southern milieu is distinct from theirs as his tragic consciousness is informed by an existential awareness of isolation and expatriation with religious overtones. However, Styron's southern background does provide him an insight into modern human condition.

Although the presence of certain *leit motifs* in his first novel *Lie Down in Darkness*, and his subsequent writing has led critics to view Styron as an adherent of the Southern school of fiction, he has expressed himself quite unmistakably against such easy categorisations. Resenting the attitude of the critics who tend to interpret an author "in accordance with their preconceived notion of what school he belongs to" instead of getting to know "what makes him fresh or genuine," Styron emphasizes the importance of "a single writer's mind and his individual spirit" to produce literature that has universal character.[7] He refuses to posit himself in the Southern school and believes that his people "would have behaved the way they did anywhere," irrespective of the place they came from.[8] Styron, however, adds that he does not mean to repudiate his Southern background completely. Though he admits that the South presents itself as powerful material, he warns against the complacent attitude that mere local colour would suffice for art.[9] The Southern writer has to go beyond the themes that may provide a marked regional pattern for his fiction.

These statements would not, however, put Styron outside the Southern tradition completely. He has told Robert Morris that there is a strong pull in his work to explain or express certain Southern biases, sympathies and apprehensions.[10] He has made a distinction between Southern regionalism and his own work "which is Southern, but perhaps not regionally southern."[11] In spite of the urge for a more cosmopolitan sense of direction, he concludes that he is never quite able to divest himself of the Southern thought.

The South has made Styron aware of the ironic mode that reality is larger than one's private consciousness and that man can "rise to human tragedy and embody genuine comedy."[12] He has learned to focus from this vantage point to gauge the depth of human tragedy from the perspective of traditional values. However, unlike Faulkner he makes use of the Southern part "without becoming nostalgically involved in it."[13]

The Southern quality of Styron's work appears to exemplify what Rubin has defined as "a way of looking at the nature of human experience" and it includes the assumption that to maintain order and stability the individual must be a part of a social community, yet that the ultimate authority that underlies his conduct, is not social but moral."[14] The crisis of conflict between the individual's moral urge and the societal demands implicit in the Southern tradition has enabled Styron to come to terms with the mood of post-World War II generation.

Styron in a way amplifies his experience of the Southern tradition into a larger matrix—the modern human condition—emphasising that "much of my experience has been formed from other backgrounds—the North, Europe."[15]

III

Styron has realised the affinities between American and European literatures in the context of man's deracination and despair. He has made his views clear on the obligation of modern writer in his commitment to life. He asserts the fact that faithlessness and despair that have fallen to the lot of modern writer were no different in nature for Dostoevsky, Marlowe or Sophocles. Despite a few characteristic "new horrors," every age has "the fleas of life" and also "nice little delights" forming its core. The main problem of art for Styron presents itself as "just one word—life."[16] A writer has to hold fast to the invariables of life, and never allow himself to be overwhelmed by a sense of chaos without. Even if the writer living in an age of spiritual bankruptcy has failed to exploit his predicament any more than Sophocles and Dostoevsky, he does experience the compelling need to know what it means to exist in a war-ridden world. His intense experience is realised in the writing born of "some strong interior need." Styron believes that this would impart "substance to and perhaps even explain all the problems of the world without even knowing it."[17]

As he belongs to the generation which has known Hitler, Hiroshima, and Korea, Styron finds himself in a world traumatised by war with the shocking recognition that it is the condition of life. Wanton violence, dehumanising alienation from the self and society characterise the experience of man in the post-war world. This awareness has found its expression and thematic unity in the imaginative fiction of the period. The image of modern man in fiction has become familiar as that of the outsider or the picaresque saint. The new literature concerns itself with values which emerge from the spiritual chaos of the individual. Its accent is on the quest for love and freedom while it asserts the importance of man's struggle against the nihilistic void left by the disappearance of the traditional values. Writing between the two world wars Eliot gave expression to the ominous situation caused by "the complete dislocation of values";

> We are obviously at the end of an age oppressed by the sense of corruption and decay, and fearful of the kinds of change which may come, since some change must.[18]

The end of an age did come with the World War II spelling "the Doomsday alternatives of nuclear extinction or dehumanized survival,"[19] disrupting the traditional values.

In his *Irrational Man* William Barrett refers to the predicament as the recurring theme of modern fiction and yet asserts that the very realisation of one's own spiritual poverty is a positive conquest by the spirit.[20] He feels that it is the obligation of modern artist to address straight to "the vacuums created by the recession of our former patterns of belief and seek his belief there."[21] Modern literature discovers its material in the spiritual chaos created by the loss of traditional patterns of belief. The contemporary novel is not, however, content with a sad analysis of man yielding to the nihilistic pressures of loss, alienation and despair. It celebrates man's desperate struggle in the vindication of his final though partial triumph. The inevitable urge to affirm and the inexplicable suffering are rendered meaningful by man's quest for salvation. Howard Harper regards the contemporary fiction as the testament of desperate faith, as it grapples with man threatened by a chaotic universe without, and also by psychopathic forces deep within.[22] Man's fate assumes a desperate urgency as he is capable of salvation despite his doubts and inevitable death. He is nevertheless a stranger with a keen sense of impending disintegration. Modern writer has the tragic awareness of a desperate need to affirm and to impose an order on the spiritual dissolution. The post-war fiction reveals the urge in projecting the protagonist who makes his way through the chaos in search of a significant moral and intellectual and spiritual order which imparts meaning to his quest. Since it is possible within the limits of nihilism to discover the means to transcend it, the function of literature should be, as Albert Camus argues, "a lucid invitation to live and to create in the very midst of desert."[23] Modern literature is, in effect, intensely moral in its commitment to overcome nihilism.

IV

The need to affirm in a bid to antidote nihilistic despair has brought the modern literature very close to existentialism "which has revived the spiritual aspects of life as significant in its own right."[24] Though existentialism is symptomatic of the deep spiritual sickness of our civilization, it views man in moralistic terms and reveals the significance of the basic realities of life such as anxiety, choice, love, freedom, guilt, and conscience.

Styron's passionate moral commitment reveals a tradition of psychological and moral analysis characteristic of the existentialist mode. He has expressed his concern for the existential need of dedication to "being" threatened by nihilism. In a letter to *The Paris Review*, he makes his stance clear:

> I still maintain that the times get precisely the literature that they deserve, and that if the writing of this period is gloomy the gloom is not so much inherent in the literature as in the times. The writer's duty is to keep on writing, creating . . . he (the writer) *must* go on writing, reflecting disorder, defeat, despair, should that be all he sees at the moment, but ever searching for the elusive love, joy, and hope—qualities which, as in the act of life itself, are best when they have to be struggled for, and are not commonly come by with much ease. . . .[25]

Styron's emphasis on the search for love, joy and hope is reminiscent of Faulkner who believes that man will endure and prevail because he has "a spirit capable of compassion and sacrifice and endurance."[26] The struggle for the eternal verities of human heart in the post-war fiction has a sense of urgency as "the only recourse against radical isolation, against a terrifying sense of meaninglessness."[27] Saul Bellow endorses Simone Weil's dictum that "to believe in the existence of human beings as such is love."[28] The affirmation of love is the duty of the writer in modern wasteland. To struggle and suffer in the search for and celebration of basic human values is integral to the philosophical climate of the twentieth century.

To endure and have the "courage to Be" is the inevitable need of man in his awareness of "the great cracks in the human landscape,"[29] caused by the lack of belief. This need provides the urge for modern writers to participate in the struggle to discover for man his unique human identity in a world steadily dehumanised. Richard Lehan recognises the existentialist stance in the modern American fiction and writes:

> Sartre, Camus, Bowles, Bellow, Wright, Ellison—all are concerned with the meaning of identity in the modern world, the nature of good and evil, the possibility of fulfilment in the contemporary society the source of values in a world without God, and the possibility and meaning of action in an ethical vacuum. The new American hero is similar to the French existential hero because he shares a common world and a similar world view.[30]

While voicing the uncertainties, complexities and paradoxes rife in the field of contemporary culture, the modern American fiction asks the eschatological questions which in the past beset the religious quest. They have now become all the more acute in view of the rejection of God. The only meaningful action in an ethical vacuum is to acquire "a clear sense of the self, or of hanging on against fearful odds to an integral self, already in being."[31] The existentialist character of modern American fiction is further substantiated by the agony which informs all its characters when they confront the vapid routine of life alternating with a sense of loneliness.

Robert Detweiler finds the connection between Styron and the existentialist philosophy as being particularly intimate.[32] The pervasive existential mood had prompted Styron to create characters in his fiction which desperately struggle to invest life with meaning in a world where the unity is fragmented by irrational forces. The suffering they experience in their bid to preserve human values, and also the very extinction of the values they vindicate define Styron's tragic humanism. Though Styron believes that a whole creed can be put on the word "endure," he wants to discover if there is still place in this world for love, sacrifice and endurance.[33] The accent on love and freedom, the desperate affirmation as a counter to nihilism and the quest for values connect Styron's tragic humanism with the existentialist humanism in general and Albert Camus in particular.

Existentialism has assumed great importance after World War II as the unprecedented scale of global violence shocked human imagination. Barrett has called existentialism the philosophy of the atomic age, since the atomic explosion has become the revelation of "the dreadful and total contingency of human existence."[34]

The concern of the existentialists is, in the main, with man's basic insecurities, his bewilderment in the face of impersonal universe. Existentialism has no place for the kind of man who has been variously categorised in terms of natural sciences at the expense of the human element. It questions the implicit assumptions of functionalistic theories of man and rejects positivism, instrumentalism, pragmatism and operationalism as inadequate means "towards a rediscovery of spontaneous man in his world."[35] Existentialism analyses that part of man which the other philosophies have either ignored or failed to deal with adequately. In order to appreciate the humanistic slant of existentialism, it is necessary to review the basic tenets of Humanism.

V

Humanism recognises the value or dignity of man and makes him the measure of all things and takes human nature, its limits, or its interests as its theme. In the context of its historical meaning, Humanism is a significant aspect of the Renaissance as revealed in its endeavour to reintegrate man into the world of nature and history. The term "Humanism" has meant the education proper to man, especially the classical discipline which is believed to restore a spirit of freedom as a justification for man's claim of rational autonomy. Humanism was seen as a conscious effort to revive and develop the capacities and powers of man supposed to be lost in the Middle Ages. This was at the base of the Renaissance predilection for the classical world in preference to the medieval heritage. Humanism has always exalted man's freedom to project his life in the world in an autonomous way as expressed in the view of F.C.S. Schiller:

> Humanism in philosophy is opposed to Naturalism and Absolutism; it designates the philosophic attitude which regards the interpretation of human experience as the primary concern of all philosophizing and asserts the adequacy of human knowledge for their purpose.[36]

Humanism would place man in the centre of the intellectual universe and insist on human relevance of all science and literature. Schiller believes that in its constant reference to human life and its purpose, philosophic humanism connects itself with literary humanism.[37]

Humanism shows a great measure of confidence in man's capacity to mould or fashion his life in the world. It has upheld the superiority of the active life to the contemplative, of moral philosophy to physics and metaphysics. Renaissance humanism contributed to the birth of modern science with its belief that man as a natural being is interested in making nature his domain and would understand it with the senses.

Paul Elmer Moore and Irving Babbitt have led the movement of Neo-Humanism with its chief doctrine of "inner check" and with its stress on harmony and restraint as chief values. Babbitt has stated that "After all to be a good humanist is merely to be moderate and sensible and decent."[38] The Neo-Humanists have tried to synthesize all that is good in ancient cultures and religions while refusing to believe in a transcendental deity. In sum, the Neo-Humanism has for its fundamental element and anti-metaphysical and anti-romantic definition of man as a product of the natural and the human, and also an anti-positivistic and anti-naturalistic conception of "human law" in the place of the law of Nature, both external and internal.

"Humanism" is also used to designate Communism, Pragmatism, Personalism and Existentialism causing confusion about its precise application.[39] Sartre is aware of the confusion and he makes an attempt to define the limits within which existentialism can be seen as a form of humanism. He understands the term as having two very different meanings. In the first place, it may be a theory which upholds man as the end-in-itself. Existentialism is not humanism from this point of view as it refuses to take man as the end, since man is still to be determined. It also rejects the belief that humanity is something to which a cult could be set up. In the second, humanism may be defined in essence as follows:

> Man is all the time outside of himself: it is in projecting and losing himself beyond himself that he makes man to exist; and, on the other hand, it is by pursuing transcendent aims that he himself is able to exist. Since man is thus self-surpassing, and can grasp objects only in relation to his self-surpassing, he is himself the heart and centre of his transcendence. There is no other universe except the human universe, the universe of human subjectivity. This relation of transcendence as constitutive of man (not in the sense that God is transcendent, but in the sense of self-surpassing) with subjectivity (in such a sense that man is not shut up in himself but forever present in a human universe)—it is this that we call existential humanism.[40]

Sartre holds that this is humanism because it emphasizes that there is no legislator but man himself and that he can realize himself as truly human only "by seeking, beyond himself, an aim which is one of liberation or of some particular realisation."[41] However, Sartre's defence of existentialism as humanism stems from the intense personalism of the existential method. Existentialism could be viewed "as much a reform as a form of humanism."[42] Humanism has held that man is born "good," and his will is vitiated by corrupt theories and institutions. The humanism of the contemporary existentialists has no illusions about man's ethical certitude as it derives from a profound ethical tension. Sartre insists that nothing can redeem for man the absurdity of the world in which his is the only consciousness capable of being aware of itself. Sartre views man involved in perpetual tension as he is, never at home in the world though irretrievably attached to it. He has used two phrases to express the disjunction between man and his world: *Being-for-itself* and *Being-in-itself.* The first is a conscious being which has no fixed universal "human nature." The second is always the same—inert, silent and dead; it is oppressive and sickeningly absurd in its sheer excessiveness. In a world of *Being-in-itself* man, the *Being-for-itself*, must create his essence by the sum total of his free acts. The *for-itself* can never become the *in-itself*, as it is perpetually oriented toward the future and transcends itself from moment to moment. Man is the only manifestation of being that has within it the possibility of becoming other than he is. Man never *is* what he is at a given moment but only what he *will be* as the result of his free choice. Since man is nothing else but what he makes of himself, he experiences *anxiety* in the act of his choice as he should choose alone and without the traditional aids of conventional morality, God or an all-justifying Absolute. In a world without a God or gods man feels himself *forlorn*, and in a world in which he must act without hope of any meaning other than what he himself introduces, he feels *despair*. Realising this ever-present responsibility, Sartre has commented "man is condemned to be free."[43] He insists that in choosing for himself, man chooses for all men and the responsibility becomes all the greater as it concerns mankind as a whole. Thus Sartre's ethic of action is determined by the concept of *mauvaise foi* which is the result of the perverse effort of the *for-itself* to become the *in-itself* and escape the anguish of trying to live the authentic life. Unethical action is always characterized by *mauvaise foi.* In the concluding passage of his work *Existentialism and Humanism*, Sartre says that existentialism is optimistic in view of the fact that nothing can save man from himself including a valid proof of the existence of God.[44] In spite of his assertion to the contrary, it is evident that existentialist humanism is tragic with its constant reference to the need of choice in full awareness of responsibility in a world that has no *a priori* value. However, Sartre's definition of existentialism as humanism refuses to take man himself as an end insisting that a man is always in a state of formation. The entire theory is oriented towards *the future.* Simone de Beauvoir makes the consequences of this attitude clear when she states that "Men of today will be sacrificed to those of tomorrow because the present appears as the "facticity" that one must transcend toward freedom."[45] Sartre's interpretation of humanism appears to leave no scope for communication as he reveals that "hell is other people"[46] and that for man "his number one enemy is man."[47]

Albert Camus recognises this flaw in the Sartrean interpretation of humanism, and he directs his whole effort at reinstating the inalienable value of the present in opposition to the future. He postulates a human nature that must be respected and a terrestrial brotherhood that must be defended. He refuses to compromise the dignity of man.

Rachel Bespaloff has defined Camus's thought as tragic humanism as its sole concern seems to be with the question: what value abides for the man condemned to death in the absence of the consolations of the supernatural ?[48] The world of Camus's thought, in her view, is the world of the man condemned to death. Belonging to a generation forced by history to live in a climate of violent death and arbitrary cruelty, Camus has faced the reality of human suffering both as a part of human condition and as a result of man's inhumanity to man. Camus's effort is to find an adequate and effective humanistic ethic to take the place of the rejected religious assumptions of Christianity. He believes that man's experience of life cannot be reduced to any coherent, rational system as he has in mind a sense of the meaninglessness of man's life, the inevitability of death, man's frail mortality in the context of the 'eternal duration' of nature, and the failure of communication with other people. He is further aware of the arbitrary destructiveness and suffering caused by the natural calamities like earthquake, avalanche, flood and famine. This is the tragic human condition. In addition, he is appalled by the incredible amount of dreadful suffering inflicted on man by man, brought to the fore by the age which has known the massacre of innocent men, women and children in concentration camps and also the colossal nuclear holocaust of Hiroshima. Camus is moved by "the fact of apparently arbitrary human suffering and death, and the fact of willed suffering and death inflicted on man by men."[49] Camus asks the question whether it makes any sense to go on living once the meaninglessness of human life is fully understood and appreciated. In *The Myth of Sisyphus*, he has shown the inadequacy of traditional religious and secular ideologies to impart sense to man's life. This makes for the isolation of man as an evaluative and purposive being in a world devoid of all supports and moral certitudes. Camus calls it the absurdity of human condition. Nevertheless he maintains that suicide cannot be regarded as an adequate response to the experience of absurdity, since it is an admission of incapacity. According to Camus, man achieves his full stature only by living in the face of his own absurdity. He holds that man will assume heroic proportions living the conflict through the recognition of the meaninglessness of the universe. Camus has throughout his work warned against nihilism and stressed the importance of humanism. He has asserted that man should revolt as he is pitted against the world that negates his human identity. The call to revolt becomes a call to create as the revolt is the sustained endeavour to transform the inhumanity of the world into the image of man and to humanize what is inhuman. Camus has found a telling metaphor for the predicament of modern man in the myth of Sisyphus. Sisyphus is condemned by gods to push a heavy rock up a steep hill for ever only to have it roll down again. The futile routine goes on without end. For Camus, Sisyphus is a symbol of man's fate and his possibilities in a purposeless world, since he has by his passion for life won the great penalty: the compulsion to exert his whole being to accomplish nothing. Nevertheless Camus emphasizes that Sisyphus is superior to his fate and "stronger than his rock."[50] Camus discovers the highest human attribute in the myth of Sisyphus and thus describes its significance in conclusion:

> Sisyphus teaches the higher fidelity that negates the Gods and raises rocks. He, too, concludes that all is well. This universe henceforth without a master seems to him neither sterile nor futile. Each atom of that stone, each mineral flake of that night-filled mountain, in itself towards the heights is enough to fill a man's heart. One must imagine Sisyphus happy.[51]

Camus's interpretation of the myth is both subtle and suggestive. In his comments on the "Absurd" he has never lost sight of the sense of optimism, a passionate longing for life. Even if one grants Sisyphus happiness, it is, however, the kind of happiness that is akin to Lear's realisation that "ripeness is all." Camus suggests that human life despite its glory is in essence tragic.

The moral significance of value-nihilism is obvious as Camus tries to persuade through *The Stranger* that a positive ethic of human fraternity can be generated by a nihilistic attitude towards all values. Meursault, the hero of the novel, views the whole conventional human apparatus of moral distinctions as a kind of meaningless gibberish. In his attitude to his mother's death in a home for the aged, and in his relationship to his mistress, he reveals himself totally devoid of feeling and impervious to human touch. He kills an Arab on a sudden impulse for no particular reason, and he is condemned to death. He spurns a priest who tries to persuade him to accept the reality of his guilt and the possibility of redemption. But at the very end of the novel, Meursault, about to die on the gallows, declares his love of the world and his fellowmen and speaks of his involvement in common human fate. He scorns all traditional consolations and behavioural patterns. He confronts nihilistic void and extracts from it "a grim acceptance of life." Bespaloff comments that "Meursault directs his protest against the human lot. Amid the indifference of a world devoid of God, nothing has any importance of value, except the pure act of living."[52] To live and to affirm in the face of absurdity is the human ethic for Camus.

While Camus examines human condition in *The Myth of Sisyphus* and *The Stranger*, he probes into man's inhumanity to man and the sources of rebellion in *The Rebel* and *The Plague*. There is a discernible movement in his thought from the recognition of the importance of personal existence to the assertion of human solidarity. "The absurd" and "the rebellion" are the two key concepts in his thought: the one points to the recognition of nihilism and despair and the other to the necessity of refusal to submit to them. Camus writes that "Man's solidarity is founded upon rebellion, and rebellion can only be justified by this solidarity."[53] Rebellion is bound up with human existence as the rebel is "determined on creating a human situation where all the answers are human."[54] He further states that rebellion is inconceivable "without a strange form of love." Camus explains:

> In the light, the earth remains our first and our last love. Our brothers are breathing under the same sky: justice is a living thing. Now is born that strange joy which helps one live and die, and which we shall never again renounce to a later time. On the sorrowing earth it is the unresting thorn, the bitter food, the harsh wind of the sea, the ancient dawn for ever renewed. With this joy, through long struggle, we shall remake the soul of our time. . . . [55]

The compassion for the suffering humanity is the theme of *The Plague.* The pestilence that descends on Oran symbolises not just the Nazi occupation of France or even totalitarianism as a political system but the whole life. The novel presents a variety of reactions to the epidemic. Dr. Rieux, the organizer of the "sanitation squads," is Camus's ideal of moral action. The doctor knows that his struggle to fight the evil is an unavailing one. It can only be temporarily defeated. We read about Dr. Rieux:

> And indeed he listened to the cries of joy rising from the town, Rieux remembered that such joy is always imperilled. He knew what those jubilant crowds did not know but could have learned from books: that the plague bacillus never dies or disappears for good . . . and that perhaps the day would come when, for the bane and enlightening of men, it roused up its rats again and sent them forth to die in a happy city.[56]

In spite of this defeatist awareness that there is no final victory over nihilism, he retains his sense of humanity and his capacity for love and for happiness. The doctor is "a saint without God." A study of his character reveals certain positive human values. He symbolizes the attempt to put a constructive meaning into a meaningless existence. It is a way of asserting human dignity, human values and human solidarity. This is, in Camus's view, the positive aspect of rebellion. In the world, devoid of supernatural meaning, man has meaning because he is the one living creature that demands coherence and significance. Nihilism is no justification for various kinds of inhumanity. In *The Rebel*, Camus writes that "we all carry within us our places of exile, our crimes and ravages. But our task is not to unleash them on the world; it is to fight them in ourselves and in others."[57] Camus's attitude toward life is informed by a stubborn moral integrity and deep compassion for his fellow men. Man decides to rebel only to assert that the human society has some positive value. Camus's tragic humanism rests on human solidarity realised in the act of rebellion inspired by compassion.

In a large measure, the tragic humanism as reflected in the post-World War II American fiction, derives from Camus. Ihab Hassan recognises the impact of Camus as congenial to the American experience:

> . . . there is much in the American experience lonely, extreme and willed as it is, that invites the existential sense of man's nudity and of his self-reliance. It was not surprising, therefore, that in a world challenged by the erosion of old pieties and values, the works of certain European existentialists took hold in America. Foremost among these was Albert Camus, who found the courage, in *The Myth of Sisyphus* (1955) and *The Rebel* (1956) to face the radical incongruities of man and to affirm human dignity by rejecting in the name of lucidity, the ultimate temptations of suicide and of murder.[58]

The Camusian theme of "the courage which rises above ultimate and inevitable failure, the day-to-day love for men as they are," is "the *medical* element" which is actually felt in America.[59] Camus's humanism is regarded as "the spiritual face of American democracy."[60] The influence of Camus in America is in consonance with the stance of the best American writers who have always given concrete shape "to those tragic elements that society officially wishes to ignore, but that survive in the unspoken consciousness of many."[61]

VI

Styron is very much in the tradition of Camusian tragic humanism as he admits that "Camus has had the largest effect upon my thinking, and I have valued the quality of his moral intensity more than any thing I have found in any other contemporary."[62] Styron has not only exemplified in his novels what Hoffman characterises as "a peculiarly modern tragedy" but he has also indicated that there is an undying thirst for order. His fiction becomes a means to explore guilt and suffering in existential terms with eschatological force. He evokes the spiritual conflict of man in apocalyptic images with the overtones of Old Testament and Greek tragedy, providing an adequate form of the complex theme.

Styron's characters struggle to counter the forces of evil. They discover their identity through suffering which becomes a positive value in the knowledge of the self. Morris and Malin describe the unique perception of Styron's characters with wide range "from the realist to the mystic, from the supernatural to the lunatic, from the secular to the divine; from the private to the apocalyptic."[63] They further observe:

> Styron's people are compulsive, intense, made of a human fibre both elastic and tough. It comes as well because in some ideal way each does aspire to 'love, joy, hope,' does (in F.J. Hoffman's words) 'struggle just to *assert* one's humanness, to get over the barriers of understanding, to clear personality of obsessions. . . .' Their quest is for nothing less than a kind of grail: buried within the darker divisions of a world of conflicting change and value, to which they are drawn by its fitful incandescence, as by their own burning, ecstatic, and often tragic visions.[64]

Styron sustains the tragic tension in the human struggle as he plants his characters securely in "what is concrete, mundane, ordinary."[65]

Styron's vision is as expansive as it is deep. He takes into his fictional world a large number of human concerns to make it comprehensive. His world-view is shaped by his persistent search for a base to discover, to define and to defend man's humanity. In spite of his great faith that man will prevail, he remains the brooding Virginian who believes that "all ages are tragic, that heroism is always succeeded by tragic outcome, and that this is the human condition."[66] Dealing with men trapped by the human condition, he considers that "life is a demonstration of oppression and submission, and variations upon them."[67] Styron writes:

> I do not underestimate the difficulties, the peculiar sense of alienation and frustration and apartness which must be the agony of every modern writer; they are acute and they are real, and no amount of ringing affirmation will exorcise them out of existence. There are no writers who today sometimes do not feel absolutely *drowned.* But this is not a plea; it will be the death of writers when they exist by indulgences. The state of drowning, of bewilderment, of horror, of a sense of betrayal from all sides is possibly the healthiest situation in which a writer can find himself. . . . I believe that in literature, as in life, ripeness is all—that creativity is its own reason for being. . . . It is not the *Zeitgeist* that writes our stories for us, but human beings whom we know. . . .[68]

Styron believes that in order to examine contemporary life, the writer has to confront it with all its bewilderment and horror to understand the continuity of the self in action. He rejects generalizations and historical explanations as inadequate to interpret literature "the only reason for our existence."[69] Styron has shown concern for the human beings at various levels—in absurd situations, in rebellion and in groping towards choice and affirmation in a non-heroic and non-human world characterized by war, atomic bombs, and military institutions. He has insisted that mere reflection of disorder, defeat and despair would not in itself constitute a creative experiment.

Styron's novels deal essentially with the efforts of man to become free and to affirm his humanity in his confrontation with violence and despair. His characters follow the pattern of existential despair leading to the fearful vision of oblivion of nothingness. Yet his fiction strives for the cure of "nothing." There is, however, a psychic division and ambiguity in the very search for the cure. Man is in the society, and he is very much hemmed in by the forces beyond his control. He may turn a rebel only to face the impenetrability of walls that block his way. It generates psychic isolation on his disapproval of the things as they stand.

Barrett regards the isolation as the source of existential awakening to human worth as man learns that the solitude of the self is an irreducible dimension of human life.[70] He is solitary and unsheltered before his own death. However, man learns about himself only after some disaster or some political upheaval has revealed the basic insecurity of the human world. Man needs to be shocked by violence into the recognition of truth concerning his own existence.[71] The ubiquitous presence of violence is noticed in the work of Faulkner, Silone and Camus.[72] They have mirrored in their novels, the nihilism, the murders and the self-annihilations with remorseless fidelity. They are often accused of morbidity, but they have not chosen violence unnaturally since it has provided them an accessible means to reach the sources of human existence. The post-World War II fiction has shown a great deal of predilection for violence and suffering. Styron illustrates his search for order and human element through the means of violence in various forms. Because of his artistic involvement and integrity he is indignant at the affluent exterior of modern life which has "the almost unimaginable presence of the bomb,"[73] and he seeks sometimes to shock the reader by scenes of cruelty, rape and murder to uncover the irrational forces that lie underneath the thin comforting veneer of life. The presence of violence in Styron's fiction should be viewed against the background of contemporary fiction.

VII

The most important theme of the contemporary novel is the record of man's struggle to overcome the pressures which drive him toward anonymity, alienation, despair, and loss of the self. The psychic isolation resulting from the pressures has deprived man of his sense of significance. Rollo May in his study of the sources of violence has discovered that violence is a means to win for man a sense of significance. He writes:

> No human being can exist for long without some sense of his own significance. Whether he gets it by shooting a haphazard victim on the street, or by constructive work, or by rebellion, or by psychotic demands in a hospital, or by Walter Mitty fantasies, he must be able to feel this I-count-for-something and be able to *live out* that felt significance. It is the lack of this sense of significance, and the struggle for it, that underlies much violence.[74]

Rollo May proposes five levels of power present as potentialities in every human being's life: power to be, self-affirmation, self-assertion, aggression and violence. He explains that the failure to live out the *power to be* will result in neurosis or psychosis or violence. *Self-affirmation* is the cry for recognition as human beings care for survival *with* some esteem. *Self-assertion* emerges against attempts to thwart self-affirmation. A stronger form of reaction against the pressures to negate self-assertion results in *aggression.* In the failure of aggression, *Violence* explodes. May writes further:

> Violence is largely physical because the other phases, which can involve reasoning or persuasion, have been *ipso facto* blocked off. In typical cases, the stimulus transmitted from the environment to the individual is translated directly into the violent impulse to strike, with the cerebrum bypassed.[75]

Apart from the psychological inevitability of violence, May regards it as a necessary condition of human life. Death, he avers, is a violent act as it separates man forcibly from this life. Viewed against the fact of death, human life is a series of violent acts. He explains:

> Death is not the only violence—or violation—we must all suffer. Life is full of other violent acts. Our very birth, the necessary struggles between parent and child, the heart-rending separations from someone we love—all these are experiences in which physical and psychological violence inevitably occurs. No life is free from violent episodes as it runs its course.[76]

Death is not merely a cruel end. It is also the possibility imparting meaning to life and to love. May has shown in his study that violence is not always destructive. It becomes a constructive means in the light of man's imminent need to affirm his significance. Since violence is the web of life, it finds its reflection in literature. Death and violence have inspired the creative artists down the ages to mediate on man's mortality. The aesthetic ecstasy of the violence in great literature reveals man's mortality with a sense of immediacy. The Aristotelian catharsis of pity or terror brings man closer to his centre and also to his fellow men. Life becomes meaningful in recognising community and compassion. Violence becomes a means of understanding as it connects man and society. May quotes Jacob Bronowski to illustrate the importance of violence as a basic human need:

> The love of violence is, to me, the ancient symbolic gesture of man against the constraints of society. Vicious men can exploit the impulse, but it is a disaster to treat the impulse as vicious. For no society is strong which does not acknowledge the protesting man: and no man is human who does not draw strength from the natural animal. Violence is the sphinx by the fireside, and she has a human face.[77]

In the dialectic of the rebel and the society, the crux is that the rebel realizes that the society has given him security and developed his potentialities. Nevertheless he acutely feels its constraints that stifle him. He rebels. The violent struggle of the rebel is to transform the society into a community. This conversion is possible only by communication which implies the presence of "social interest." It is a way of relating oneself to the other "as a human being in the full meaning of that term."[78] May believes that "communication leads to community—that is, to understanding, intimacy, and the mutual valuing that was previously lacking."[79] Albert Camus emphasizes the value of rebellion as an intensely human gesture establishing community as he concludes "I *rebel*—therefore *we* exist."[80] In this context violence itself becomes a kind of communication. Violence does not always, however, establish community. Community is often imperilled by destructive violence. Violence would become constructive and establish community when it is tempered by compassion as May defines:

> Compassion is the name of that form of love which is based on our knowing and our understanding each other. Compassion is the awareness that we are all in the same boat and that we all shall either sink or swim together. *Compassion arises from the recognition of community*. . . . Compassion is the tie felt for another not because he 'fulfills his potentialities' (as if anyone ever did !). Compassion is felt toward another as much because he *doesn't* fulfill his potentialities—in other words, he is human, like you or me, for ever engaged in the struggle between fulfillment and nonfulfillment. We then surrender the demand that we be divine in order to join mankind in its suffering and its destiny.[81]

The isolation necessitates violence. Violence as an affirmative act is tempered with compassion and it establishes community. The rebel thus opts out of society and comes back to it with greater understanding and compassion. May further defines compassion:

> Compassion gives us a basis for arriving at the humanistic position which will include both power and love. Compassion occupies a position opposite to violence; as violence projects hostile images on the opponent, compassion accepts such demonic impulses in one's self. It gives us the basis for judging someone without condemning him. Although loving one's enemies requires grace, compassion for one's enemies is a human possibility.[82]

Violence and Compassion as human possibilities are interrelated in their source—man's loneliness. Jacob Bronowski says: "we are all lonely . . . we've learnt to pity one another for being alone. And we've learnt that nothing remains to be discovered except compassion."[83] Violence may be viewed as man's endeavour to break his hubristic isolation. He gains understanding and Compassion through violence.

VIII

Styron admitted that "all of my works contain violence" but also declared that pure violence repels his constitution. He views violence as an anti-pleasure and states that in art violence has to be dealt with a great deal of subtlety to make it meaningful. He notes that since violence is central to our racial experience, it is within everyone's experience and therefore "enters into our literature, into the book we write."[84] He feels that violence has become an inescapable fact for the modern writer and adds that "the violence that intrudes into my work has to do with my own knowledge of the violence that surrounds us all at this moment."[85] In fact Styron's knowledge of violence has a great deal to do with American history, and more particularly his Southern background.

American history is a long chronicle of violence reflected right from the beginning when fierce religious dissent caused the exodus from the settled European countries into America. The promised land merely presented the settlers with brutal Indian wars, hostile environment and international rivalries. The war of independence followed later by a bloody civil war only stressed violence as an inescapable fact of life. In addition, violence erupted fiercely all along the frontier beyond the settlements till the end of the 19th century. The historian Richard Maxwell Brown states that "Violence has formed seamless web with some of the noblest and most constructive chapters of American history. . . ."[86]

The South in particular has a keen sense of violence in "the lash of the slave driver, the Bowie knife of the old Southwest, the duelling pistol of the hot-headed gentleman, the rebel yell of the fire-eater, the gasoline torch of the lyncher, the fiery cross of the klansman."[87] The plantation system bred conditions of violent slave insurrections with its rigid enforcement discipline. The South has in a way become "the embodiment of violence in America."[88]

The South felt its sectional identity acutely and nurtured "a generous and often an obsessive sense of the past"[89] as the main shaper of its life, after its defeat in the civil war. Indifferent to commercial expansion and progressive optimism it chose to live "on the margin of history" and got the "perspective from the social rear."[90] Irving Howe defines the Southern myth as a story or cluster of stories that express the most fundamental experience of its people in "the fate of a ruined homeland." It has become the basic Southern subject even if the Southern writer could "enlarge it into an image of the general human situation."[91] Driven to a regional past by the reality of the twentieth-century life, the Southern writers have given evidence of "a fundamental quarrel with modern life."[92] The work of Faulkner, Caldwell, Warren and Styron is patterned in the tense admixture of tradition and modernity.

Since the South has become heavily mythologized, it exploits the fund of myth and sets up the act of violence as a metaphor of emancipation. Paul West believes that this technique has given the Southern fiction the makings of "the novel destiny"[93] in which the protagonist, as Frohock puts it, finds exit impossible except through violence to some other human being.[94] Since violence becomes man's fate, the kind of novel is in a sense tragic."

Violence has been a dominant theme in the literary tradition of the South, prominently since 1930. It has shaped the major Southern fiction writing providing it a definite thematic substratum, a mode of perception, a tone and a pattern of emotions. The probing into human condition through violence as a means is noted in the major writers like William Faulkner, Erskine Caldwell and Thomas Wolfe. The recent Southern writers like Robert Penn Warren, Flannery O'Connor, Truman Capote, Carson McCullers and William Styron have exploited violence in its psychological and physical manifestations, viewing its emergence as a necessary concomitant of man's questioning of his humanity and his being, as he is affected by the discoveries of science, technological developments and political upheavals in the twentieth century. In their work the concern for the region and its history brings into focus the conflict between the religious fundamentalism and rapid industrialization as the characters struggle passionately for identity in the face of the gaping nihilistic void. The conflict takes on the contours of violence.

IX

The Southern fiction has always shown its pre-occupation with violence as a means of recognition of relationship between man and the world. Faulkner has viewed violence as emerging from the fact that man cannot know the meaning of his acts and yet he is responsible for the consequences. Violence in Faulkner becomes a complicated mode of ethical questioning as he makes use of it to express his horrified awareness of human corruption and vulnerability illustrated in the disintegration of the Southern traditional life. Malcolm Cowley, in his introduction to the *Portable Faulkner*, says that the violence of Faulkner's work is "an example of the Freudean method turned backward, being full of sexual nightmares that are in reality social symbols. It is somehow connected in the author's mind with what he regards as the rape and corruption of the South."[95]

Caldwell adopts the technique of caricature which reveals violence as a temporary deflection of perception. He hardly invests it with enough significance to render it as a permanent revelation of human nature or the region. Since Caldwell manipulates characters and incidents to place their created world as merely contingent upon social circumstances his technique of grotesque enlargement fails to probe the tragic implications of human existence. The theme of horror often becomes an end itself and never gets transformed into pity.[96]

Thomas Wolfe's fictional world introduces man as limited and imprisoned in self. His sense of frustration, failure and defeat becomes an inevitable factor. Man's impulsive demands for definition in the midst of his doom surge up in a frenzied assault on the system to break it open into order and integrity.

Violence in Wolfe functions explicitly as a revelation of what Pamela Hansford Johnson calls "a young man's socialism based on the generous rage, the infuriated baffled pity."[97]

The thematic importance of violence in Faulkner and Caldwell could be understood as an attempt towards the expression of meaning of life. In Wolfe it becomes tangential. While Caldwell simplifies life in grotesquely distorting human dignity and significance by making man an instinctive creature of food and sex, Faulkner makes use of violence and distortion to discover and celebrate man's indestructible spirit and his capacity to endure. Robert Penn Warren adopts violence as a means of self-discovery. The urge to know one's own self becomes a source of violence as it causes the inescapable conflict between the characters and the world. The progressive self-discovery marks the effectiveness of violence. In Warren violence becomes a constructive mode of human action. He believes that violence alone would provide an insight into the tension between the contrarities like good and evil, ideal and actuality, the self and non-self. Warren holds that the attempt to effect a separation between the act and the ideal ends in violence, as it negates the unity of life. He has concern for "moral order and moral violence which sometimes coincide with physical order and violence in the world of men."[98] His concepts of violence and order become meaningful in Southern terms.

Flannery O'Connor uses violence to rip the thin cover of pretence that masks human nature. She reveals the twisted demonic selves from an intensely religious point of view. O'Connor's conscious purpose is to reveal the need for grace in a grotesque world without transcendent context. She believes that "violence is strangely capable of returning my characters to reality and preparing them for their moment of grace."[99]

Styron appreciates the fictional concerns of the South as revealed in Faulkner, Caldwell, Wolfe, Warren and O'Connor. He believes with Faulkner in man's endurance and values Warren's emphasis on self-discovery and O'Connor's religious concerns. Styron's characters grapple violently with themselves and their environment because of these compulsions, implicit in the Southern history. Like Caldwell and Wolfe he reveals social evils through the technique of the grotesque, though the social criticism in Styron is not as explicit as it is in his compatriots.

Styron's characters violently rebel and stubbornly hope. In a violent world they act, suffer and become compassionate. Humiliated in a world which negates and destroys, they affirm the human values—hope, pity, love and compassion. Robert Morris and Irving Malin notice this "double-vision" and comment on the protagonists of Styron's fiction. In their passionate search for human values Peyton (*Lie Down in Darkness*) commits suicide, Captain Mannix (*The Long March*) persists in small, and unnoticed martyrdom, Cass Kinsolving (*Set This House on Fire*) plunges into the gaping hell of Sambuco, and Nat Turner (*The Confessions of Nat Turner*) causes the horrendous blood bath in Southampton country.[100] Styron's tragic humanism springs from the fact that in a violent world compassion flows from suffering alone, and that one has to suffer the loss of human values in the struggle to preserve them.

The theme of compassion is intimately bound with the humanistic thought. The unfoldment of human potentialities is possible by establishing a relationship with the world and by cultivating an attitude of productive love towards man himself. Erich Fromm emphasizes that one can be related to "the human core" of another only through love, and that the unfolding of the human in man is chiefly through human solidarity.[101] The American novelists have shown deep concern for the attitudes and beliefs of the individual that further or retard his attempts at integration. They have probed into the elemental forces of life to reveal man in his naked humanity by planting him in situations which demand the fullest participation of his vitality in response. They put to test man's pattern of values in such irreducible moments of life. Hawthorne's Arthur Dimmesdale in *The Scarlet Letter* represents the fierce spiritual struggle to free himself from psychic isolation and rediscover the warmth of human relationships. Chillingworth's remorseless persecution of Dimmesdale violates "the sanctity of human heart." Hester returns to the society which cast her out. Her integration with fellow-men through love and compassion has been at the heart of Hawthorne's humanism. Melville's *Moby Dick* presents Ishmael as a symbol of redemption as he reveals reverence for life through his friendship with Quecqueg. Ahab's fury excites admiration but it becomes counter-productive and nihilistic. Melville suggests that man finds the faith to overcome despair in his capacity to reach out to his fellow-beings through purposive relationship. Mark Twain's *Huckleberry Finn* unfolds Huck's ethical awareness and Jim's inherent dignity in a series of experiences which enable them to relate to "the human core." The classical American fiction is consecrated to a study of "the whorls of man's moral impulses."[102] It has always judged man against a background of authentic morality.

However, the modern American novel has come under severe indictment for its treatment of the theme of compassion. Edmund Fuller has expressed his reservations about the use of the word "compassion" in regard to the sloppy sentimentality of modern novels.[103] He objects to elevating a mood into philosophy as is done, for instance, in such contemporary works as Steinbeck's *The Wayward Bus*, Jone's *From Here to Eternity*, and Mailer's *The Deer Park*. Fuller is disappointed with "the inverted pathos" for the morally degenerate as "a kind of counter-puritanism." He is convinced that "no valid compassion can exist without a moral framework."[104] He believes that Dostoevsky's *Crime and Punishment* or *The Brothers Karamazov* would be impossible in the absence of a dramatic conflict of evil and good. He explains:

> In short, the new compassion is the denial that men and women are what their consistent, voluntary (and involuntary) patterns of action make them. The element of true tragedy and compassion—the fall from a standard responsibility however extenuated, repentance and the struggle for rehabilitation—are not in this philosophy.[105]

It is true that contemporary American fiction employs the sources of pathos rather than of comedy or tragedy. Though tragedy is inevitable in man's life as the reach of his awareness goes beyond his grasp, it also gives the knowledge that there is no way out. In the absence of a sense of the reach extending beyond man's grasp, the tragic passion cannot be sustained and there is then the descent into pathos. The generous view of life unmistakably evident in modern fiction cannot exclude the degenerate from its compassionate understanding. Once the flow of compassion is vitiated by the enquiry whether the social outcastes deserve it or not, it degenerates into a condescending pity.

Fuller bemoans the woeful lack of adequate materials for tragedy in the modern world and deplores the complete disappearance of a moral framework in the French existentialist movement which has its impact on the work of such serious writers as Ralph Ellison, Norman Mailer, Paul Bowles and William Styron. He fails to appreciate the moral preoccupation of modern novel as it is neither tragic nor human in his view. It is difficult to share Fuller's total rejection of the existentialist fiction on moral grounds. Camus, for example, has continued his quest for meaning beyond *The Myth of Sisyphus.* His concern is whether one could be a saint without God. He believes that there is no shame in preferring happiness, but at the same time he avers that "it may be shameful to be happy by oneself."[106] Camus discovers the values of life and happiness lost in the holocaust of our age by placing happiness in the reconciliation of man and nature and in the movement of the heart towards fellowmen. Doubrovsky comments that Camus is the man "who knows that once the plague has come he must reenter the city,"[107] since man is doomed "the day he forgets to love—in spite of evil and suffering—this creation without a creator."[108]

Like Camus, Styron realises that man's isolation is tainted with *hubris,* and that compassion alone liberates him. In his novels he has led the protagonists gradually from Peyton's doomed isolation and suicide to Nat's serene compassion and martyrdom. Styron has always taken care to project his characters against a moral framework. They never lapse into "blurred self-pity." The unflagging tragic tension in his novels renders Styron's compassion valid in the moral realm as it "recognises the sharing of all human guilt, the potentiality of evil in the most blameless."[109] Styron deals with the theme of compassion in its traditional and psychological complexity. In his novels one may visualize the pattern that man negates order within and without through violence, and suffers. Suffering chastens him and the cathartic act is completed in compassion anti-doting hubristic isolation. Styron is among those who "can express despair without succumbing to it, and they can question and deny the validity of traditional consolations without denying the traditions of the human spirit."[110]

XI

There is a need to study in depth Styron's tragic humanism in relation to the dominant themes: Violence and Compassion. The interrelation of violence with compassion alone would make it meaningful in the human context and realisable in art. This study makes an attempt to reveal the significance of the two antithetical elements in human existence as revealed in Styron's novels.

The major American critics like R.W.B. Lewis, Frederick J. Hoffman, Alfred Kazin—to name only a few—have paid considerable critical attention to Styron's art. However, the controversy caused by *The Confessions of Nat Turner*, largely in relation to its sociological significance, has not only generated bitter acrimony in the heat of discussion, but also provoked quite a few critics to view Styron's work in a new perspective and study its pattern and thematic concerns. Marc L. Ratner in his *William Styron* has made an attempt to examine Styron's main techniques and ideas, and to trace his progressive artistic development through his four novels. Styron's existential and Christian predilections have been explicated in Robert Detweiler's *Four Spiritual Crises in Mid-century American Fiction* and Robert H. Fossum's *William Styron* respectively. David D. Galloway has explained Styron's novels in the light of the concept of "Absurd" in *The Absurd Hero in American Fiction.* Ihab Hassan has made perceptive comments on the patterning of Styron's first two major novels in his *Radical Innocence.* While these detailed analyses have shown excellent insights into Styron's themes and technique, a large body of periodical criticism has addresssed itself to his "Southernness" exclusively. Mention may be made of John W. Aldridge, Elizabeth Janeway and Harvey Swados who have found Styron under the heavy impact of William Faulkner and the Southern mode of fiction writing.

One gets the impression that the Styron scholarship has all along shown specialist approach to one particular thematic aspect of his work: its Southernness, its religious sensibility or its sociological significance. The scholarship has, in the process, failed to view these different aspects forming Styron's integral vision as he consistently makes use of his Southern background to illuminate modern human predicament the better. Styron has placed his characters in the South to counterpoise violence and compassion inherent in the regional life pattern and to structure a fable of man's journey in the modern wasteland, committed to his fierce affirmation of humanity.

Louis Y. Gossett's *Violence in Recent Southern Fiction* devotes a short chapter to Styron, and Ratner comments briefly on Styron's violence. Yet Gossett and Ratner have tended to regard violence as emerging in isolation chiefly because of the writer's background. They have not noticed the meaningful interaction of violence and compassion as the core of Styron's tragic humanistic stance in the larger context of modern human condition. This study proposes to integrate Styron's Southernness and his treatment of violence and compassion in his novelistic pattern to the humanistic concerns of modern fiction by analysing his *Lie Down in Darkness, The Long March, Set This House on Fire* and *The Confessions of Nat Turner*.

NOTES

1. Peter Matthiessen and George Plimpton, "The Art of Fiction," *Paris Review*, 2 (Spring 1954), rpt. in Malcolm Cowley, ed., *Writers at Work: The Paris Review Interviews* (London: Mercury Books, No. 29, 1962), p. 244.
2. Frederick J. Hoffman, *The Art of Southern Fiction: A Study of Some Modern Novelists* (Carbondale: Southern Illinois University Press, 1967), p. 14.

3. Robert Heilman, "Southern Temper," in *South: Modern Southern Literature in Its Cultural Setting*, ed. Louis D. Rubin Jr., and Robert D. Jacobs (Garden City, N.Y.: Doubleday Dolphin Books, 1961), p. 48.
4. Louis D. Rubin Jr., p. 12.
5. Ibid., p. 25.
6. Ibid.
7. *Writers at Work*, p. 244.
8. Ibid.
9. Ibid., p. 245.
10. Robert K. Morris, "An Interview with William Styron," in *The Achievement of William Styron*, ed. Robert K. Morris and Irving Malin (Athens: The University of Georgia Press, 1975), p. 27.
11. Ibid.
12. Louis D. Rubin, Jr., "Notes on the Literary Scene: Their own Languages," *Harper's Magazine*, 230 (April 1965), p. 175.
13. Marc L. Ratner, *William Styron* (New York: Twayne Publishers, 1972), p. 135.
14. Louis D. Rubin, Jr., *William Elliots Shoots a Bear: Essays on the Southern Literary Imagination* (Baton Rouge: Louisiana State University Press, 1975), p. 230.
15. Harriet Doar, "Interview with William Styron," *Red Clay Reader*, Vol. I (1964), p. 26.
16. *Writers at Work*, p. 250.
17. Ibid., p. 252.
18. T.S. Eliot, "Literature and the Modern World," in *American Poetry and Prose*, ed. Norman Forester, 4th ed. Part II (Boston: Houghton Mifflin Company, 1962), p. 1366.
19. Jonathan Baumbach, *The Landscape of Nightmare: Studies in the Contemporary American Novel* (New York: New York University Press, 1965), p. 2.

20. William Barrett, *Irrational Man: A Study in Existential Philosophy* (New York: Doubleday, 1958), p. 46.
21. Ibid., p. 153.
22. Howard H. Harper, *Desperate Faith: A Study of Bellow, Salinger, Mailer, Baldwin and Updike* (Chapel Hill: The University of North Carolina Press, 1967), p. 197.
23. Albert Camus, *The Myth of Sisyphus*, trans. Justin O' Brien (Harmondsworth: Penguin Books, 1975), p. 7.
24. Robert Detweiler, *Four Spiritual Crises in Mid-Century American Fiction* (Gainesville: University of Florida Press, 1968), p. 46.
25. *Paris Review*, 1 (Spring 1953), pp. 9-13.
26. William Faulkner, "The Stockholm Address," in *William Faulkner: Three Decades of Criticism*, ed. Frederick J. Hoffman and Olga W. Vickery (New York and Burlingame: Harcourt, Brace and World, 1963), p. 348.
27. Robert Gorham Davis, "In a Ravelled World Love Endures," *The New York Times Book Review*, 26 December 1954, p. 13.
28. Saul Bellow, "Distractions of a Fiction Writer," *The Living Novel* (New York: Macmillan, 1957), p. 20.
29. Frederick J. Hoffman, "William Styron: The Metaphysical Hurt," *The Art of Southern Fiction: A Study of Some Modern Novelists*, p. 14.
30. Richard Lehan, "Existentialism in Recent American Fiction: The Demonic Quest," *Texas Studies in Literature and Language*, I (Summer 1959), pp. 181-202, rpt. in *Recent American Fiction: Some Critical Views* (Boston: Houghton Mifflin Company, 1963), p. 64.
31. R.W.B. Lewis, "American Letters: A Projection," *Yale Review*, 51 (December 1961), pp. 211-226.
32. Robert Detweiler, p. 13.
33. William Styron, "The Prevalence of Wonders," *Nation*, 176 (2 May 1953), pp. 370-371.
34. William Barrett, p. 65.

35. Ulrich Sonneman, *Existence and Therapy* (New York: Grune and Stratton, 1954) as quoted by Hazel E. Barnes in "Humanistic Existentialism and Contemporary Psychoanalysis," in Edith Kern ed., *Sartre: A Collection of Critical Essays*, Twentieth Century Views (Englewood Cliffs, N.J.: Prentice-Hall, 1962), p. 155.
36. F.C.S. Schiller, "Humanism," *Encyclopaedia of Religion and Ethics* (New York: Charles Scribner's Sons, 1955), VI, p. 830.
37. Ibid.
38. Irving Babbitt, *Rousseau and Romanticism* (New York: Macmillan, 1919), p. xxi.
39. Nichola Abbagnano, "Humanism," *The Encyclopaedia of Philosophy* (New York: Macmillan and The Free Press, 1967), p. 72.
40. Jean-Paul Sartre, *Existentialism and Humanism* (London: Eyre Methuen, 1973), p. 55, trans. Philip Mairet.
41. Ibid., p. 56.
42. Philip Mairet, "Introduction," *Existentialism and Humanism*, p. 15.
43. *Existentialism and Humanism*, p. 34.
44. Ibid.
45. Quoted by Serge Doubrovsky in "The Ethics of Albert Camus," *Preuves*, No. 116 (October 1960), 39-49, rpt. in Germaine Bree, ed., *Camus: A Collection of Critical Essays*, Twentieth Century Views (Englewood Cliffs, N.J.: Prentice-Hall, 1962), p. 78.
46. Ibid., p. 79.
47. Ibid.
48. Rachel Bespaloff, "The World of the Man Condemned to Death," in *Camus: A Collection of Critical Essays*, p. 92.
49. John Cruickshank, "Introduction," *The Plague* (London; Hutchinson Educational, 1967), p. xi.
50. Albert Camus, *The Myth of Sisyphus*, p. 109.
51. Ibid., p. 111.
52. Rachel Bespaloff, p. 95.

53. Albert Camus, *The Rebel* (London: Hamish Hamilton, 1960), p. 27.
54. Ibid.
55. Ibid., p. 273.
56. Albert Camus, *The Plague*, p. 281.
57. Albert Camus, *The Rebel*, p. 268.
58. Ihab Hassan, "Since 1945," *Literary History of the United States: History*, ed. Robert E. Spiller et al, 3rd ed., rev. (New York: Macmillan, 1963), p. 1416.
59. Serge Doubrovsky, "Camus in America," in *Camus: A Collection of Critical Essays*, p. 18.
60. Ibid.
61. Ibid.
62. Brodin, *Presences Contemporaines* (Paris, 1964), pp. 210-11 as quoted in Ratner's *William Styron*, p. 136.
63. Robert K. Morris and Irving Malin, eds., *The Achievement of William Styron*, p. 3.
64. Ibid.
65. Ibid., p. 4.
66. Robert K. Morris, "An Interview with William Styron," *The Achievement of William Styron*, p. 34.
67. Ibid., p. 36.
68. William Styron, "Introduction," *Best Short Stories from the Paris Review* (New York: E.P. Dutton, 1959), pp. 9-16.
69. Ibid.
70. William Barrett, p. 34.
71. Ibid.
72. R.W.B. Lewis, *The Picaresque Saint: Representative Figures in Contemporary Fiction* (New York, Philadelphia : Lippincott Company, 1959), p. 27.
73. William Styron, "My Generation," *Esquire 70* (October 1968), pp. 120-24.
74. Rollo May, *Power and Innocence: A Search for the Sources of Violence* (New York: W.W. Norton, 1972), p. 37,

75. Ibid., p. 43.
76. Ibid., p. 171.
77. As quoted by Rollo May, p. 219.
78. Ibid., p. 247.
79. Ibid.
80. Albert Camus, *The Rebel*, p. 221 (emphasis added).
81. Rollo May, p. 251.
82. Ibid., p. 252.
83. Jacob Bronowski, *The Face of Violence: An Essay with a Play* (Cleveland: World, 1967), pp. 161-62.
84. "Violence in Literature," *A Symposium in American Scholar*, 37, 3 (Summer 1968), p. 485.
85. Ibid., p. 486.
86. Richard Maxwell Brown, "Historical Patterns of Violence in America," in *The History of Violence in America: Historical and Comparative Perspective*, ed. Hugh Davis Graham and Ted Robert Gurr (New York: Praeger, 1969), p. 75.
87. Charles R. Anderson, "Violence and Order in the novels of Robert Penn Warren," *Modern American Fiction: Essays in Criticism*, ed. A. Walton Litz (New York: Oxford University Press, 1967), p. 273.
88. Ibid.
89. Irving Howe, "The Southern Myth and William Faulkner," *Dissent*, 3, No. 4 (Winter 1951); rpt. in Henning Cohen, ed., *The American Culture* (Hyderabad: ASRC, 1972), p. 43.
90. Ibid., p. 44.
91. Ibid.
92. Ibid., p. 45.
93. Paul West, *The Modern Novel*, Vol. 2 (London: Hutchinson University Library, 1963), p. 284.
94. Wilbur Merrill Frohock, *The Novel of Violence in America*, 2nd ed. rev. and enl. (Dallas: Southern Methodist University Press, 1958), pp. 6-7.

95. Malcolm Cowley, "Introduction," *Portable Faulkner* (New York: The Viking Press, 1946), rpt. *William Faulkner: Three Decades of Criticism*, p. 104.
96. Louise Y. Gossett, *Violence in Recent Southern Fiction* (Durham, N.C.: Duke University Press, 1965), p. 29.
97. Pamela Hansford Johnson, *The Art of Thomas Wolfe* (New York: Charles Scribner's Sons, 1963), p. 151.
98. Charles R. Anderson, p. 280.
99. Flannery O'Connor, *Mystery and Manners*, ed. Sally and Robert Fitzgerald (New York: Noonday, 1970), p. 112.
100. Robert K. Morris and Irving Malin, "Vision and Value: The Achievement of William Styron," *The Achievement of William Styron*, p. 3.
101. Erich Fromm, *Man for Himself: An Enquiry into the Psychology of Ethics* (New York: Holt, 1947), pp. 100-01.
102. Stanley T. Williams, "Nathaniel Hawthorne," *Literary History of the United States: History*, p. 420.
103. Edmund Fuller, "The New Compassion in American Novel," *Man in Modern Fiction* (New York: Random House, 1958), p. 35.
104. Ibid., p. 38.
105. Ibid., p. 37.
106. Albert Camus, *The Plague*, p. 190, trans. Stuart Gilbert.
107. Serge Doubrovsky, p. 84.
108. Ibid.
109. Edmund Fuller, p. 34.
110. David Galloway, *The Absurd Hero in American Fiction* (Austin and London: University of Texas Press, 1974), p. x.

2

Lie Down in Darkness

Styron's *Lie Down in Darkness** deals with the violent disintegration of Southern family in the absence of love, as Milton Loftis, the alcoholic father, his wife Helen, the neurotic mother and Peyton, the nymphomaniac daughter fail to find a meaningful centre in life and drift. Milton and Helen confront a grim sense of nullity. Peyton ends her life violently. Styron explores the aridity of human life by chronicling the events of the doomed family in the grip of death, decay and pervasive violence.

The critical preoccupation with Southern elements has put *Lie Down in Darkness* at a disadvantage. Its artistic complexity and thematic depth have been hardly touched upon since important critics have chosen to read the novel as being entirely meaningful in the context of its Southern background. Aldridge appears to be fairly representative of this view, as he squarely puts it as "a novel of place" adding that the novel "must be

***Lie Down in Darkness* (London : Jonathan Cape, 1970). All subsequent references in parantheses are to this edition.

judged in terms of its successful evocation of its place."[1] He has painstakingly listed the elements which would stamp it as genuinely Southern. It cannot be denied, however, that there are quite a few trappings lent to it by the Southern background. Yet *Lie Down in Darkness* goes beyond the regional frontiers. Styron is conscious that the thematic concerns of the novel would be severely constricted within the regionalistic framework. He has told David Dempsey:

> I wanted to write a novel that has more than regional implications. I wanted to avoid the ancestral theme, too—the peculiar, inbred and perverse types that Faulkner, Caldwell and Southern writers have dealt in. At the same time I didn't want to exploit the old idea of wreckage and defeat as a peculiarly Southern phenomenon. Elements of this are in this book, but they're part of the people rather than the place. I like to think that my story could have happened in Massachusettes just as well as Virginia.

The people are more important than the place, even if the landscape imparts them identity and provides them a perspective. Realized in art, the achieved identity of the characters determines the universal validity of their shaping destiny in the fictional form. The particularity individuates and when treated with competence, it validates the universality of experience. Alfred Kazin recognizes the implicit paradox of the regional writing and comments:

> perhaps it is only the writer who knows that men are not the same everywhere, who believes that each human being is original and has a soul—perhaps it is only such a writer who will stick to his birthplace as if the whole of life were as much there as anywhere.[3]

A significant aspect of Styron's art lies in transcending the local colourist's view of things without foregoing the advantage of Southern tradition. Styron makes use of the Southern background to dramatize the fundamental human relationships rooted in a particular place to illuminate modern man's predicament in his doomed though heroic struggle to win for himself a dignified fate. Certain conflicts and constraints such as the elements of fundamentalist religion, regionalist guilt and the contrast of races, did give Styron a few stylistic nuances, structural devices and thematic priorities. He has admittedly kept his background "as an intangible feeling," and integrated his regionalistic predilections to impart the novel a complex vision of life which is disconsolate and tragic. The theme of *Lie Down in Darkness* is the despair implied in the human condition with its impossible quest for resurrection and redemption in the midst of temporal negation and mortality.

Besides Southernness, Faulkner's impact on Styron has loomed large in the critical analyses of *Lie Down in Darkness.* William Van O'Connor felt that the novel would be entirely different "if Faulkner had not written *The Sound and the Fury* and the other novels."[4] Malcolm Cowley has complimented Styron on his making the Faulknerian impact most personal in his novel.[5] Robert Gorham Davis has discussed at length the close kinship of *Lie Down in Darkness* with *The Sound and the Fury.* He writes:

> Styron's Peyton resembles Faulkner's Quentin in more than name. Not only does each commit suicide, but the suicides are preceded by the same thought and symbolic action. Both have weak fathers with similar philosophies of life. In both families there are mentally defective siblings and a loyal Negro female servant. Both end to the refrains of a Negro gospel meeting. Both are naturalistic accounts of a doomed family.[6]

Styron's competence in handling the characteristically Southern theme of disintegration, decay and death in his novel has prompted Ihab Hassan to conclude that Styron has learned to put Faulkner's legacy to his own service.[7] Even in the structure of the novel Styron's indebtedness to Faulkner is considered evident. In addition to the plot, characters, themes, interior monologues, flashback technique and several points of view make the novel in a great measure Faulknerian.

But these many similarities should not be allowed to shadow the original fictional approach to reality that Styron has displayed in his novel. Though he found Faulkner "the hardest to shake off," and despite the fact that the early parts of his novel were so imbued with the senior novelist's style that he had "to go back and rewrite them completely," Styron was able to outgrow Faulkner's influence. This is evident in the method of his character creation which is distinct from that of Faulkner's. He argues that his characters would have to stand or fall as individuals without any reference to the Southern background. Thus steering himself clear of the Southern regionalism, he welcomes Faulkner as his mentor only so far as he gives his 'complexity' without his 'confusion.'[9]

The question of Faulkner's influence on Styron should lead one to examine in detail the extent to which Styron departs from Faulkner in responding to the Southern material in his writing. To ignore this would be simply to re-read Faulkner in Styron without any effort to view the pattern which renders *Lie Down in Darkness* different in its presentation of human experience.

Faulkner has viewed man's identity as integral and meaningful in the traditional concept of community. He has recorded the disintegration of Southern community with the advent of modern urban life. The process of social dissolution has deprived all institutions of their accepted and established roles leaving only attitudes intact. Though the Southern writers of Styron's generation share these attitudes born of institutions now no longer in existence, they are distinguished by their independent way of looking at human experience. The awareness of this subtle shift in the Southern backdrop, makes Louis D. Rubin, Jr. comment that *Lie Down in Darkness* is "not a Faulknerian tragedy at all."[10] It is for him a literary exploration of the surviving attitudes to impart meaning and order to modern human experience not identical with traditional Southern life.[11]

Lie Down in Darkness though based on the Southern pattern finds its dramatic causes in the present, while the power of *The Sound and the Fury* stems from a region and its history. Styron's novel has created "its own kind of tragedy," albeit the fact that it derives from the same literary and cultural tradition that rendered Faulkner's fiction "so profoundly moving."[12] Further Styron would not lend his characters dynastic scope like Faulkner in *The Sound and the Fury*. He would not create a separate fictional region, like "Faulkner Yoknapatawpha or Conrad's Costaguana," but exploits the Southern landscape as it is. He has never given much importance to the pervasive myth of the fall of the Old South. *Lie Down in Darkness* does not deal with some ancient curse upon the land after the Faulknerian mode, its concern is with "ill-defined neurosis which afflicts the collective psyche."[13]

However, Faulkner's impact on Styron is evident in the strategy he has adopted to manipulate time. Discussing at length Faulkner's metaphysic of time, Sartre comments that his problem was to get beyond chronological time and use the present as "full of holes through which past things fixed, motionless, and silent invade it."[14] Sartre believes that for Faulkner "The present does not exist, it becomes." The function of the present is limited to the context to which it reveals the past and gives it a pattern. This pattern would impose a meaning on the past. Sartre compares Faulkner's vision of the world to that of a man sitting in an open car and looking backward. The formless shadows and quivering points of light that rise on either side of him become trees, men and cars only afterward when he has a little perspective.[15]

Styron has admitted that his greatest problem in writing his first novel has been "the progression of time."[16] The chronological arrangement of events, he has felt, would never reveal the psychological complexity, and in addition it would mean the easy evasion of the chaos that is man's lot. The chaotic life cannot be given an authentic form in a plain narrative order. *Lie Down in Darkness* chronicles emotional, social and spiritual chaos that one confronts. The whole narrative gets into focus only in retrospect as it traces events leading to the final catastrophe unravelling the inexorable march of forces beyond the control of characters caught up helplessly in an irredeemable situation. Structured on a funeral procession, *Lie Down in Darkness* attempts a pitiless exploration into the paradox of man's search for reality and the inevitable fact of human destruction. Suicide, Death and Burial provide the pattern of existence and characters are caught up in the vortex of destructive forces. Styron leaves no room for freedom and therefore, no hope for redemption in the rigid scheme he has chosen especially in manipulating the technique of time in his novel.

Peyton's death in the present gives the still point to probe into the past and in the process one becomes aware of the nihilistic "Nothing" in life. The cracked time in the novel is revealed "in flashbacks and flashbacks within flashbacks."[17] In tackling the "progression of time" Styron has come close to the dark doom of *The Sound and the Fury*. Faulkner's past has no chronological order, its structure is born of "certain impulses and emotions." The importance of the present is left to the shift of time. It may or may not be consequential since its level can be determined only by its own intrinsic value and its relevance to your lives. The present, for Faulkner, is only a stasis to peer into the past, and the future has no significance. The past puts out the present and the future. Faulkner's man, therefore, is a prisoner of "mutilated time."

Styron in his *Lie Down in Darkness* has made his characters captives of the same predicament. Victims of inexorable past, Milton, Helen and Peyton have failed to arrive at some sort of personal identification. There is no projection into future in the closed frame of the novel with its emphasis on "beginning in which middle and end are swallowed."[18] The complicated chronology of the novel becomes a structural device to support "the crushing accumulation of violence."[19] The past has not only determined the present of Milton Loftis and his wife Helen, it has also swallowed their future. The fact of death in the present unveils the past leaving no scope for future. Time in *Lie Down in Darkness* also is ordered by "certain impulses and emotions." It makes the characters prisoners of the past put down by the heavy frame of unbearable reality. It directly conforms to the post-modern sensibility that has witnessed the rupture of the old laws of cause and effect. The structure of *Lie Down in Darkness* negates the causal connections between past, present and future. It gives the unmistakable impression that there are no physical, emotional, psychological or ethical directions in the absence of an "organic nexus."[20] It has no sense of passing time eroding communal value as in Faulkner. While Faulkner unfolds the past Styron reveals the present. The past for Styron may throw light on the present, but it cannot redeem. The world of *Lie Down in Darkness* is unredeemed by time. The struggle for freedom is beset with violence in various forms. Towards the end the novel dramatizes the juxtaposition of violence and compassion with the suggestion that compassion alone is the effective humanizing force in the spiritual wasteland with its decay, disaster, incest and insanity.

Styron brings to the fore the elements of violence and compassion on three levels each revealing the other in greater relief: the Southern background, the psychological complexity of the characters and finally the symbolic suggestion of compassion as a counter to violence. He has exploited the violent imagery of the Book of Revelation to uncover the spiritual nullity of contemporary life in the hopeless Loftis tragedy which is significantly enacted in the simultaneous explosion of the atomic bomb with Peyton's suicide.

II

The Southern background should not, however, be mistaken for the easy parallels so often provided in the analyses of *Lie Down in Darkness.* Styron employs the Southern background for its rich evocative and symbolic significance. He suggests that the Southern microcosm has macrocosmic scope with the epitaph chosen from *Urn Burial.*

> And since death must be the *Lucina* of life, and even Pagans could doubt, whether thus to live were to die; since our longest sun sets at right decensions, and makes but winter arches, and therefore it cannot be long before we lie down in darkness, and have our light in ashes; since the brother of death daily haunts us with dying mementos, and time that grows old in itself, bids us hope no long duration;—diuturnity is a dream and folly of expectation.

The title of the novel deriving from the seventeenth century reflection on death and inevitable decay turns on the ruin, destruction, violence and gloom within the Southern context. Styron telescopes the times past with the present, and the concrete present situation with human condition in general. He takes care to introduce the South of the Tidewater Virginia to convey the decay and dissolution:

> Riding down to Port Warwick from Richmond, the train begins to pick up speed on the outskirts of the city, past

> the tobacco factories with their ever-present haze of acrid, sweetish dust and past the rows of uniformly brown clapboard houses which stretch down the hilly streets for miles, it seems, the hundreds of rooftops all reflecting the pale light of dawn; past the suburban roads still sluggish and sleepy with early morning traffic, and rattling swiftly now over the bridge which separates the last two hills where in the valley below you can see the James River winding beneath its acid-green crust of scum out beside the chemical plants and more rows of clapborad houses and into the woods beyond.

The corruption introduced by the technological progress has not however driven away the gloom of the background. Its weedy growth and mounds of garbage invoke the horror of decay:

> Halfway between the railroad station and Port Warwick proper—a distance altogether of two miles—the marshland, petering out disconsolate, solitary clumps of cat-tails, yields gradually to higher ground. Here, bordering the road, an unsightly growth of weeds takes over, brambles and briars of an uncertain dirty hue which, as if with terrible exertion, have struggled through the clay to flourish now in stunted grey profusion, bending and shaking in the wind. The area adjacent to this stretch of weeds is bleakly municipal in appearance: it can be seen from the road, and in fact the road eventually curves and runs through it. Here there are great mounds of garbage; a sweet vegetable odour rises perpetually on the air and one can see—from the distance fairly iridescent – whole swarms of carnivorous flies blackening the garbage and may be a couple of proprietary rats, propped erect like squirrels, and blinking sluggishly, with mild, infected eyes, at some horror-stricken Northern tourist. (67)

The South is not merely a spiritual wasteland. Styron emphasizes the nature of violence embedded in the history of the region. Milton remembers his father saying, ". . . always remember where you came from, the ground is bloody and full of guilt where you were born and you must tread a long narrow path toward your destiny." (73) The sense of corruption, decay and violence makes it a land of death. At one stage Milton realises the enveloping sense of death:

> Death was in the air; he thought briefly of his father, of Maudie; but wasn't autumn the season of death, and all Virginia a land of dying? (188)

The spiritual isolation is realized further as Peyton and Dick Cartwright make love in an old bungalow:

> And it was as if their tension and their exhaustion—namely Peyton's grief and lostness, her despair—had begun to communicate itself to the house. Amid those ancient rooms which carried even to this day, along with the radio, electric lamps and modern chairs, a sort of minor squalor of ancestral piety—old canes carved from hickory, many years dead, long before the war began, and a pulpit-sized, rat-chewed Bible, and ante-bellum novels still dusty and uncut in their cases, and faded Christian lithographs of the Apostles and the Ascension and a swooning Susanna—amid all these they wandered, bearing with them, like an anachronistic odour, their peculiarly modern despair. . . . (235)

The South manifests modern despair in its faded gloom and fallen ideals. Beneath the veneer of adolescent aristocratic culture and elaborate ceremonies, it is not hard to find that life in the South has lost its cohesive human factor – love. Berger tells Peyton in New York:

> . . . it is symptomatic of that society from which you emanate that it should produce the dissolving family. . . . I know you say symptomatic not of that society, but of *our* society, the machine culture, yet so archetypal is this South with its cancerous religiosity, its exhausting need to put manners before morals, to negate all *ethos*—Call it a *husk* of a culture. (363)

The archetypal background of the South is manipulated to reflect modern spiritual desiccation. Fossum perceives that "the disrupted temporal structure of *Lie Down in Darkness* reflects the spiritual and emotional disruption of a world in which property has replaced morality, lust has replaced love, and carefully tended houses and lawns disguise the spiritual disorder of their middle-class owners."[21] Peyton, the product of the spiritual crisis, believes in the regeneration of the South:

> Why couldn't they realize certain obvious truths: that the South was benighted, maybe, and the people filled with guilt, but didn't they see that this was the very tragic essence of the land, that it was still going through its upheaval, still shattered by conflicts, that it was improving, rising from the ruins, and that when it emerged, it would be a greater place for its very ordeal ? (332)

The uncertain promise in the remote future cannot, however, save Peyton from the imminent dissolution. Recognising the elements of the Southern background in the patterning of characters in *Lie Down in Darkness*, John W. Aldridge comments that the causes of dissolution are inevitable.

> Behind Milton's father-guilt and incest-guilt is the whole Southern blood-guilt. Behind Helen's jealousy and Puritanism is the timeless Southern gentlewoman madness, the madness that comes from too much inbreeding, too much Negro fear, too much sexual neglect. Behind Peyton's father-complex is a century of paternalism and man-hatred and sexual masochism.[22]

Although it is difficult to agree with Aldridge as he sums up the entire motivation in terms of the South, it should, however, be conceded that the implacable forces finding their source in the South have rendered the personal relationship in the novel violent and destructive.

The Loftises have no inner strength to rise above their weaknesses in the absence of an established social structure of values. Their failure becomes all the more remarkable and glaring because the South in the background acts as a reminder of another standard to measure the violence that change has wrought.

III

Charlotte Kretzoi, in her perceptive critical analysis of the novel, has called *Lie Down in Darkness*, a classic tragedy.[23] Its significance as a work embodying tragic vision cannot be lost sight of in the seemingly impenetrable texture of the numerous reflections, interior monologues and sub-plots. Concealed by the device of conscious rhetoric throughout the novel lies the simple fact that it deals with the failure of love and inevitability of disintegration in the lives of three doomed characters of the tragedy: Milton, Helen and Peyton.

The psychological complexity of characters in *Lie Down in Darkness* finds its violent release in various episodes that culminate in Peyton's suicide. Besides the Southern *husk* of culture and its failure to provide an ethical centre, the pattern of life in the novel is much too complex as infidelity, vengeful love and refusal to grow, render its world static. Hassan describes *Lie Down in Darkness* as

> a story of a husband unfaithful to his wife, a mistress unfaithful to her husband, a girl unfaithful to the man she marries. It is the story of a woman, Helen, who can love only what she can control—her crippled daughter, Maudie, or the childish part of her husband, Milton; of a man whose sensuality is merely a form of dependence on Dolly; and whose love, for Peyton, can never become sensual; of a girl who frantically needs a husband, Harry, precisely because she loves her father, and who hates the mother who is viciously jealous of her. These ambivalences of love are created by a man-child, girl-woman, and mother-neuter—the images of reversion in the novel are legion—who bind the family in a circle of guilt.[24]

Imprisoned in a circle of guilt, the characters remain fixed in their tragic inability to love. While Milton and Helen are trapped like wingless birds driving violence inward and becoming masochistic, Peyton makes frantic efforts to break the barriers and becomes a willing victim of self-destruction.

Peyton had committed suicide by jumping from a loft in New York. The news of tragedy descended on Milton with a shattering effect confounding him beyond all hope.

> It (the coffin) would come, bearing with it, too, evidence of all his errors and of all his love—because he loved his daughter more than anything—and the thought suddenly struck him—that of meeting her this morning, silent, invisible within a coffin—filled him with horror. (12)

He feels isolated in his sorrow as Helen refused to go with him to receive the coffin at the station. Milton goes there with his mistress Dolly. In the fifteen minutes that he should wait for the train and later following the slow-moving hearse from the station to the cemetery Milton explores the past in an effort to *endure*. The Ibsenic narrative technique unveils the impending sense of doom. The slow and gradual revelation of each chapter furthers the onward movement as each discovery adds to our understanding of the present predicament till the texture of the memories illuminates the entire past leading to the irrevocable disaster in the foreground. Milton peers into his cumulative experience to discover the cause of Peyton's doom. Unfolding his alcoholic, guilt-ridden and indulgent mind he tries unsteadily to feel the cause of his misfortune in his pitiful weakness, in his many acts of omission and commission and also in the sins of tradition.

Milton has never felt the compelling need to face reality; for him fate and circumstance are "words which all his life he had never quite understood." (11) Rich marriage has made him totally dependent on his wife's money and he has surrendered the possibility of his success in his chosen field, law or politics for the price of untroubled ease in life. His sense of helplessness becomes acute when his first child Maudie is born physically and mentally defective. His guilt is sharpened as he develops incestuous attachment for his second daughter Peyton. His neglect of his crippled first daughter Maudie compounds his guilt. In her masochistic love for Maudie, Helen despises her husband and hates her beautiful daughter Peyton. The three-cornered relationship becomes destructive. Milton has gone through life as pointlessly as he has gone in search of his daughter Peyton in a drunken haze. He never gathers himself to confront the nightmare of his failure. In the death of Peyton he realises that "his deposit . . . on all of life's happiness had been withdrawn in full and his heart had shrivelled like a collapsed balloon." (101) Milton digs deep into his memory only to promote his sense of guilt. In his youth he was guilty of jilting a socially inferior girl. He neglects Maudie dying in Charlottesville hospital, he goes to search for Peyton holding in a drunken state a confederate flag as "a trophy without honour." (207) It was a futile escape "from the colossal responsibilities." In his futility feeling "like a bug wriggling upside-down on the floor" he realises that his guilt born of his affair with Dolly Bonner has become nightmarish "like something monstrous and heavy and unutterable, prowled about his bed at night." (248) After Maudie's death Milton goes back to Helen "in a convulsion of necessity." (248)

> . . . there's something to be said for honour in this world where there doesn't seem to be any honour left. I thought that may be happiness wasn't really anything more than the knowledge of a life well spent, in spite of whatever immediate discomfort you had to undergo, and that if a life well spent meant compromises and conciliations and reconciliations, and suffering at the hands of the person you love, well then better that than live without honour. (244)

This masochistic submission brings him isolation worse than death. When Milton comes to the brink of self-knowledge, Helen fails him. She refuses to say *yes*, to forgive, love and affirm. Recalling his tender moments with her, Milton wonders:

> Why hadn't something important happened, then ? It was as if he—yes, she, too; how could he tell ?—had just tried too hard. No one knows when the heart's eye opens; theirs had opened wide for a moment and had gazed each at the other, then blinked shut as quickly. (159)

Imprisoned in his own self and shut out by grief Milton has collapsed to lie down in darkness.

Because of Milton's inability to act and to come out of his shell the psychological tension accentuates internal violence.

Its force is felt as Styron reveals compassion toward Milton castigating him, nevertheless, for his self-pity and waste.

> A man so accomplished, he reflected, might achieve as much as great men, give him patience and a speck of luck; though his road slopes off to a bitter sort of doom—and the wind, blustering down the night through chill acres of stars, suddenly made Loftis feel cold, and his life a chancy thing indeed—he has had his moment, a clock-tick of glory before the last descent. You know this man's fall: do you know his wrassling ? (260)

The understanding of Milton's wrassling is evident in Styron's "suspending of judgment in compassion."[25] He lets internal violence build up till Milton is brought to realise the fact of his enclosed existence with *No Exit*. Milton confronts the horror at Peyton's wedding:

> Across the room he sees Peyton break away from the young lieutenant, her arm crooked at the elbow in a curious, disjointed way, . . . He wishes to go to her side, to talk to her alone, and explain. He wants only to be able to say: forgive me, forgive all of us. Forgive your mother, too. She saw, but she just couldn't understand. It's my fault. Forgive me for loving you so.
>
> But at this moment, when he suddenly sees Helen, white with fury, throw a coat over her shoulders and go out on to the porch with Carey Carr, he knows that explanations are years too late. If he himself could love too much, only Helen could love so little. (292)

In a life which is devoid of love and forgiveness, the awareness of nullity is much too oppressive. Violence explodes finally outside the chapel where his daughter's body lies. Milton fails in his efforts to evoke compassion in Helen and involve her. The melodramatically violent frenzy of Milton becomes compulsive:

> 'Why have I wanted you ?' he shouted. 'Because you're the only thing left ! That's why ! My God, don't you see ? we're both sick, we need to make each other.——' (387)

Helen fails to understand Milton's agony, and he bursts out in mad fury:

> Why, God damn you, don't you see what you're doing ! With nothing left ! Nothing ! Nothing ! Nothing ! (387)

The metallic clang of 'Nothing' in the final scene is the commentary on the relentless force of violence that has led the family to ruin. Milton's weakness is reflected in his desperate need. He needs Dolly, he needs Peyton and he needs Helen. He desperately clings to props of one kind or another. His acute awareness of "Nothing" has made him the man who "has gazed so long into the abyss that the abyss has begun to gaze back at him." (243) Neither violence, nor compassion provides him a way out.

Milton is irredeemably weak. Robert Gorham Davis feels certain that a strong novel cannot be written about weakness especially when the causes of the weakness are ill-defined, also in the absence of characteristic sensibility and ideas.[26] Styron has, however, succeeded in making Milton's dangling comment on man's helplessness and his inescapable sense of responsibility, projecting his failure as a sign of human vulnerability.

The conflict between Milton and Helen has hardly any dramatic potentialities. It would not give scope for the tension of values in contrast. Helen is cold and her attitude towards her daughter's death is shockingly unchristian. Her obsession with order would not leave room for departures however small, from the rigid routine. Her very life pattern excludes love, compassion and forgiveness. She remembers that "she had wanted the future to be like a nice, long. congenial tea party, where everyone talked a little, danced a little and had polite manners." (274) Although the death of Maudie and the suicide of Peyton bring her the awareness that she was "a mother no longer and that I shall never be a mother again" (22) she refuses to give in. Helen's rigidity could be explained in terms of her unresolved sexual attachment to her father. Her love for Maudie, the perpetual child, is symbolic of her own brand of sex-less love. Peyton's beauty and youth cause her the bitterest anguish. Her monstrous preoccupation with 'all that business about evil' generates violence which is both psychological and physical. Her assertion that "I know what sin is" with her claim that "In knowing that I'll always be superior to you," makes knowledge the equivalent of power to crush Milton. Her speech reveals her incredible emptiness with the personal pronouns "*I*" and "*me*" providing "the fiction of a center."[27] Peyton knows Helen's incapacity to love and affirm, and she also recognises the fact that Helen's hate is all-consuming:

> You know, I suspect you've always hated me for one thing or another, but lately I've become a symbol to you you couldn't stand. . . . You hate men, you've hated Daddy for years, and the sad thing is that he hasn't known it. And terrible thing is that you hate yourself so much that you don't hate men or Daddy but you hate everything, animal, vegetable and mineral. (313)

Helen's psychological violence is revealed through her dreams caused by her bitter anguish over Milton's affair with Dolly. She dreams "one corpse in particular, faceless like the rest, head down in the shadows, with its legs—suppurating, clotted by a swarm of sucking, avid flies—unmistakably Dolly's." (229) Helen's anger, jealousy and hatred turn the festivities of the family into nightmarish experiences. At Peyton's wedding Helen's anger overpowers her and she explodes in a violent frenzy:

> With her arms at her side stiff as sticks, only her head moved and her blue, crazy eyes: It was like watching an adder, thought the doctor; surely she was ready to strike. None of the other guests seemed to have noticed her, and this fact too, increased his feeling of impending peril: of a snake which lies tranquil, cold as ice, save for its head motionless at the rim of some thicket, prepared as if by divine intuition to bite not the wary but the unaware. (306)

Helen's violence is the result of her stunted love. Her refusal to say 'yes' and affirm leads to the disintegration of lives of Milton and Peyton, besides causing a huge emptiness to come over her. Towards the end she confronts "nothingness" and darkness engulfs her,

Milton identifies himself with Peyton and indulgently endorses her free life. Helen identifies herself with Maudie and she accuses Milton and Peyton of grave irresponsibility towards her. Milton desperately longs for the return of his adolescent college days and refuses to confront the present. Helen withdraws herself into her fancied innocent childhood with her father protectively watching over her. Helen's world collapses with the death of Maudie and Peyton's death shatters Milton's. In spite of the tragedy they fail to respond to each other with compassion. Milton seeks out Dolly. Helen reaches Carey Carr. Their inward "nullity" manifests outwardly as they meet briefly at Peyton's grave.

Milton's footlessness and Helen's emotional aridity victimise their daughter Peyton. She becomes the pivotal character through which Styron puts to test the concepts of responsibility, guilt and judgment.

Styron devotes about seventy pages to Peyton's interior monologue as a climax to his novel. It is not merely a brilliant technical achievement, but a device to illumine what the novel is about. The epigraph of *Lie Down in Darkness* quoted from *Urn Burial* comes into sharp focus when Peyton pointedly makes use of the passage keeping the vital phrases intact.

> I pray but my prayer climbs up like a broken wisp of smoke: *Oh my Lord, I am dying*, is all I know, and *oh my father oh my darling*, longingly, lonesomely, I fly into your arms! . . . Myself all shattered, this lonely shell ? Perhaps I shall rise at another time, though I lie down in darkness and have my light in ashes. (386)

The epigraph of the novel and Peyton's prayer sum up the fate of the doomed characters.

Peyton is a victim of the domestic tragedy. Her life has lost its centre in the failure of Milton. Helen's uncompromising hate leaves no scope for her to come back home.

> I've got my own reasons for coming home. I've wanted to be normal. I've wanted to be like everybody else. There old folks wouldn't believe that there are children who'd just throw back heads and howl, who'd just *die*, to be able to

> say, 'well now my rebellion's over, home is where I want to be, home is where Daddy and Mother want me.' (269)

Shut out from home and denied love she feels adrift "without anything to pull me back to earth again." Her search for meaning leads her deeper into crisis:

> What's wrong? Why is happiness such a precious thing? What have we done with our lives so that everywhere we turn—no matter how hard we try not to—we cause other people sorrow ? (37)

Her search for answers brings the knowledge that the key to happiness is "being sort of dumb." Styron uses sexuality of reflect the tortured feelings of Peyton and also to objectify her fall from innocence. He dramatizes Peyton's act of sexual surrender to Dickie, the first of her many affairs of promiscuity, as the symbolic fall from innocence:

> Sleeping, he took her in his arms; she drew away. A dog barked across the wintry fields. There was dance music and later, Mozart, a song of measureless innocence that echoed among lost ruined temples of peace and brought to their dreams an impossible vision: of a love that outlasted time and dwelt even in the night, beyond reach of death and all the immemorial, descending dusks. Then evening came. Arms and legs asprawl, they stirred and turned. Twilight fell over their bodies. They were painted with fire, like those fallen children who live and breathe and soundlessly scream, and whose souls blaze forever. (237)

She has lost her paradise of innocence, and her initiation into adult world through sex is tortured and painful, and it finally facilitates her advent into her Hell, an absolute isolation. Her promiscuity is an expression of her realisation that her father had failed her, and later her husband Harry was unable to be a father-lover. Retaining the innocence "by divorcing the intent from the act"[28] she reflects on what has brought her to the brink of self-destruction.

> Oh, I would say, you've never understood me, Harry, that not out of vengeance have I accomplished all my sins but

> because something has always been close to dying in my soul, and I've sinned only in order to lie down in darkness and find, somewhere in the net of dreams, a new father, a new home. (380)

She wants the cessation of violence and guilt. She decides to walk into a dark closet and lie down there only "to wake in another land, in a far, fantastic dawn." Before her suicidal plunge from a twelfth storey bathroom window, she buys a clock imagining a quiet life in its brass womb:

> In my clock Harry and I would be safe from flies for ever; they'd drum about overhead blackening the sky, trying to get in, poking their noses through the skylight; we'd see the bearded prisms of their faces, the scowls; we'd be secure for ever, guarded by chrome and immutable timeless steel. (342)

Peyton has struggled violently against the irrationality of the universe and hoped for a smooth ordered world. The chaotic experience shatters her dream and she wistfully worships the inside of the clock:

> I went back to the windowsill and got the clock. I cupped my hands around it, looking at the dots and hands, which shone with a clear green light in the darkness: we have not been brought up right, I thought, peering down into the alarm hole: there in the sunny grotto we could coast among the bolts and springs and ordered, ticking wheels, riveted to peace forever. Harry would like to know; rubies he'd love and cherish, in that light they'd glow like the red hats of Breughel dancers. I could hear the screne and steady whir, held it closer to my ear for the ticking, an unfitful, accomplished harmony—perfect, ordered, whole. (345-46)

Peyton realises that her life without a centre cannot be made harmonious through alcohol or sex. The irrationality could be negated only by violence. She commits suicide.

The tragedy of Peyton stems from failure of love. Styron connects sex inevitably with violence and absence of love. The repetition of phrase "Lie Down in Darkness" in the novel evokes the contemplation of death, vanity of the world and the absence of hope of Christian immortality. Styron uses the phrase also to mean the death of sexual love, and the failure of understanding and compassion. He presents the psychological conditions which generate violence through Milton and Helen, and Peyton acts out the violence in her dreadful physical act.

Galloway believes that *Lie Down in Darkness* presents "a group of absurd situations."[29] The situations in the novel are violent as well. The use of violence goes deeper into the very structure of the novel with its imagery and polysyllabic words reflecting human tragedy in describing the drunken love-making of Peyton and Dickey boy, in uncovering Helen's insanity through her grotesque nightmares, in Peyton's agonizing interior monologues. The interior monologue expresses Peyton's apocalyptic experience. It creates the sense of incessant movement. The violently emotional and physical progress of the monologue is in sharp contrast with the dull pace of the hearse to the cemetery at the beginning of the novel. Peyton's promiscuity with its violent urge drives her in the end to her suicidal jump, creating a whirl of energy without a centre. The violence is reinforced by the atomic devastation of Hiroshima and Nagasaki. The disjointed and dissociated moments of the past crowd irrationally into the explosive present. The violent energy is explicitly indicated in the imagery of the frenzied monologue. Her guilt of incestuous feeling haunts her in the images that surface, especially the flying birds:

> There were birds in my mind, landbound birds whirling about, dodos, and penguins and cassowaries, ostriches befouling their lovely black plumes, and these seemed mixed up with Bunny. (342)

The birds symbolize purity and freedom. They also become "big birds" noiseless and flightless standing for the violent negation of her aspirations and finally they become the avenging furies of her unconscious guilt with Milton whom she endearingly calls "Bunny." The violent energy is also evident in her sense of drowning which is a symbol of orgiastic forgetfulness and also of renewal.

> I was beginning to drown some; the water not so much within me as if swallowed, but around me, not touching me, with the shimmering quality of vagrant but surrounding thick light. It seemed to lap at the windows, the mirror, making the air opalescent and somehow milky; yet it was not this water which threatened me so but my own mind: the water remained, like the birds, detached and even aloof, upon the boundaries of my consciousness a submarine wall persistent, but without menace: I wanted not to think about it. (352)

Since for Peyton "guilt is the thing with feathers," she realizes the futility of her efforts to retain innocence and to experience love. She has to lie down "somewhere in the desert topography of her mind," with no hope of survival or renewal. Peyton's monologue reveals spiritual vacuum that has become an agonising fact of human existence, She has to face the final darkness of self-destruction. Milton, Helen and Peyton are enmeshed in the net of failure to love and say, "yes."

IV

Lie Down in Darkness rises above the narrow confines of domestic tragedy as Styron suggests the atmosphere of violence in the world at large. Harry fails Peyton, but he is not insensitive to the horrid human condition in the world reduced to shambles by the bomb dropped on Hiroshima. He tells Peyton:

> There are a lot of things I'd like to talk about. Do you realize what the world's come to ? Do you realize that the great American commonwealth just snuffed out one hundred thousand innocent lives this week ? There was a time, you know, when I thought for some reason—may be just preserve your incomparable beauty—that I could spend my life catering to your needs, endure your suspicions and your mistrusts and all the rest, plus having to see you get laid in a fit of pique. I have other things to do. (378)

Harry is convinced that in the face of the overwhelming universal tragedy personal failures and agonies do not matter.

He struggles hard to hold fast to the undying hope that the wholesale destruction would not stamp out from human breast the spirit to endure. He embodies his vision in the portrait of the old man he was painting:

> In greys, deep blues, an ancient monk or a rabbi lined and weathered, lifting proud, tragic eyes toward heaven; behind him were the ruins of a city, shattered, devastated, crumbled piles of concrete and stone that glowed from some half-hidden, rusty light, like the earth's last waning dusk. It was a landscape dead and forlorn yet retentive of some glowing, vagrant majesty and against it the old man's eyes looked proudly upward, toward God perhaps, or perhaps just the dying sun. (375)

The picture is a comment on the wasteland which man has created by his demonic violence. There is still hope that man would nevertheless look upward, and toward heaven. The prospect is bleak, since it may as well be the dying sun that he would ultimately confront. The ambiguity is subtle in its juxtaposition between the inescapable violence and failure of compassion.

Styron further brings the juxtaposition in the Negro carnival described toward the end of the novel. The Southern gentry represented by the Loftises has gone to pieces. The Negroes endure and find salvation through their simple faith. The failure of Carey Carr, the official representative of the Church, is due to the fact that he has no sustained vision to redeem the disintegrating Loftis family. The violence is much too beyond his power to check. On the contrary, the Negroes of the novel affirm because of their capacity to love and to believe. Carey Carr is of the secular world which has rationalized God out of existence. The Negro evangelist Daddy Faith can promise "de word of your God shall stand forever." (399) Styron has put suggestively the Daddy Faith baptismal ceremony close after the burial of Peyton as an evocative symbol of redemption of Peyton's life shattered by violence. Daddy Faith brings a message of hope and renewal. Ella Swan and La Ruth, the Negro servants of the Loftis household find in the baptismal rites the element of rebirth in contrast to Peyton who has merely the feeling of drowning and fails in her life to find "a new father, a new home." Ella and La Ruth feel cleansed and purified through the baptismal rite, and also cry in fulfilment, "you, Daddy ! Daddy Faith ! You loves us ! You, Daddy !" (397)

Rubin, however, feels that Styron has "a much bleaker pessimistic observation"[30] that religion would become ineffective in direct proportion to the intelligence and sophistication of the believer. Religion would function as a morality only in the case of the superstitious and the ignorant. Carey Carr fails while Daddy Faith succeeds. The Loftises disintegrate while Ella and La Ruth affirm.

Styron is not indulging in an analysis of the much discussed problem of religion being effective or effete in the modern age. He has used the epilogue as a symbolic comment on the Negroes' power to love, understand and endure, through Ella whose "face wore the passive look of one who has seen all, borne all, known all and expects little more, of either joy or suffering. . . it was because her outlook on life was basically tragic." (389) There are several undertones in the scene which ironically throw into relief what has gone wrong with the Loftises. Ella and La Ruth take care of a little girl who has missed her mother in the crowd waiting for Daddy Faith. She is restored to her mother finally. But Peyton is lost irretrievably. Peyton's feeling of drowning is contrasted with the simple Negroes ducking in the water at the carnival feeling cleansed and purified. The Loftises confront "Nothing" while a sterile thunder rumbles over the cemetery. In contrast their Negro maids shout in triumphant exultation facing the sea "yes, Jesus ! I seen Him ! Yeah ! Yeah ! (400) The Negro carnival scene is symbolic affirmation of compassion against the violence and suffering that beset the Loftis family. It contrasts life with death, and spiritual regeneration with the nihilistic void. Further the role of Negro maids is not just peripheral. Styron has carefully structured the seemingly casual comments of the Negro maids to shed light on the malady or curse that afflicts the family. Ella Swan and La Ruth witness all the incidents both major and minor and comment passively and objectively revealing the tragic impact of every event. They assume the role of chorus in piecing together several situations right from the start to unfold the doom of the cursed family which parallels the Greek tragedy in its hopeless disintegration. Ella Swan uncovers the background of the tragedy at the very beginning, while waiting for Peyton's coffin: "Train gonna come soon. Peyton comin' on de 'leven-fo'teen. Po' Precious lamb." Besides emphasizing Peyton's innocence, she moans benediction deepening the gloom, "Lawd God bless us Jesus." (14) Negroes in droves appear again in the middle of the novel "laughing and sweating, carrying between them paper banners—DADDY FAITH BRINGS LOVE TO US—" They seem to be "seeking some pagan redemption in the waters of the Congo." (237) The presence of Negroes going in procession for a carnival with their primitive faith intact is in sharp contrast to the predicament of Carey Carr "like a missionary isolated among hostile natives" and Helen who cries "Fatigue." The sterility is further contrasted as the chapter which begins with the suggestion of the baptismal waters and goes on to describe the spiritual bankruptcy of the Loftises and Carey Carr (all white) ends:

> There was a crackle of a thunder. She gazed up from her kleenex. If was an odd sight. Emerging from the chapel, her hair blown by the wind, Helen stood cool and erect on on the steps, one hand lightly resting on Carey's arm. Beside her—though Dolly couldn't hear his words—Loftis was saying something. His eyes had the horror filled, yearning look they had had all day. Then—and a pang of grief such as she had never known before struck her heart—she saw Helen turn abruptly and smile, with a word to Loftis. She couldn't see the rest. Carey got in the way; for no reason at all he made the sign of the cross, and far off to the east the thunder rumbled and rolled, came nearer. It began to rain. (324)

The suggestion of the cross linked with the fact of rain emphasizes the need of faith and redemption vouchsafed for Negroes and denied to the whites hopelessly lost.

Harry Miller, Peyton's painter-husband, is a Jew. Styron brings in Harry the Jew along with the Negro maids to suggest their undying affirmation, their violent persecution notwithstanding. While the two persecuted races last, the modern

Loftises disintegrate because of their inability to love and to endure.

Though Harry's role is minor in the novel, his comments become part of an epilogue to the Loftis-tragedy. Since he belongs to the race that has survived the holocaust, he can very well speak of 'the desperate faith.'

Harry suggests affirmation through his painting. He wants "to paint and paint and paint because I think that some agony is upon us. . . I want to crush in my hands all that agony and make beauty come out, because that's all that's left, and I don't have much time. . . ." (378)

Harry the Jew, and the Negro maids exemplify the power of compassion as they represent the two most persecuted races. They have experienced violence, endured suffering and are therefore compassionate through their understanding. The epilogue is a counter to the epigraph from the *Urn Burial.* Styron has structured in the epilogue a richly suggestive and evocative scene.

Galloway, however, feels that there is no room in *Lie Down in Darkness* for "the kind of positive, creative force"[31] that Harry represents. Ratner similarly recognises its violent and fatalistic nature and calls the novel "Styron's Euripidean tragedy."[32] Both of them seem to ignore the fact that violence in *Lie Down in Darkness* is checked and subdued by compassion. Though tragic tension emerging from the doomed conflict in the novel has the fatalistic ring of a Greek drama, it veers towards what W.H. Auden has elsewhere characterized as "Christian tragedy"[33] because of its force of compassion. Auden describes the Greek tragedy as the tragedy of necessity which arouses in the spectator the feeling "what a pity it had to be this way." Christian tragedy, he explains, is the tragedy of possibility, "what a pity it was this way when it might have been otherwise."[34]

Lie Down in Darkness suggests the possibility of redemption in Milton and Peyton, though Helen is beyond hope because of her destructive pride. Peyton hints at it when she tells her father that if he had some guts and Helen a soul, she would have come back home averting the tragedy. (269) The novel finally leaves the impression that "it might have been otherwise." The fatalistic force of violence is shot through with compassion.

In his next novel *The Long March*, Styron examines with sharper insight the inbuilt violence in human organisation which overpowers the forces of compassion revealing the horror of tragic existence.

NOTES

1. John W. Aldridge, "In a Place Where Love Is a Stranger," *New York Times Book Review*, 9 September 1951, p. 5.
2. David Dempsey, "Talk with William Styron," *New York Times Book Review*, 9 September 1951, p. 27.
3. Alfred Kazin, "Faulkner in His Fury," in *Modern American Fiction: Essays in Criticism*, ed. A. Walton Litz, (New York: Oxford University Press, 1967), p. 178.
4. William Van O'Connor, "John Updike and William Styron: The Burden of Talent," in *Contemporary American Novelists*, ed. Harry T. Moore (Carbondale: Southern Illinois University Press, 1964), pp. 205-21.
5. Malcolm Cowley, "The Faulkner Pattern,' *New Republic*, 125 (8 October 1951), 19-20.
6. Robert Gorham Davis, "The American Individualist Tradition: Bellow and Styron," in *The Creative Present: Notes on Contemporary Fiction*, eds. Nona Balakian and Charles Simmons (New York: Doubleday, 1963), pp. 111-41.
7. Ihab Hassan, "Encounter with Necessity: Three Novels by Styron, Swados, and Mailer," in his *Radical Innocence* (New York: Harper and Row, 1966), pp. 124-52.
8. David Dempsey, "Talk With William Styron", p. 27.
9. Peter Matthiessen and George Plimpton, "The Art of Fiction," *Paris Review*, 2 (Spring 1954), pp. 42-57; rpt. in Malcolm Cowley, ed., *Writers at Work: The Paris Review Interviews* (London: Mercury Books, 1962), p. 246.

10. Louis D. Rubin, Jr., *The Faraway Country* (Seattle: University of Washington Press, 1963), p. 209.
11. Ibid.
12. Ibid.
13. Jan B. Gordon, "Permutations of Death: A Reading of *Lie Down in Darkness*," in *The Achievement of William Styron*, eds. Robert K. Morris and Irving Malin (Athens: The University of Georgia Press, 1975), p. 103.
14. Jean-Paul Sartre, "Time in Faulkner: *The Sound and the Fury*," in *William Faulkner: The Decades of Criticism*, eds. Frederick J. Hoffman and Olga W. Vickery (New York: Harcourt, Brace and World, 1963), p. 228.
15. Ibid.
16. Malcolm Cowley, ed., *Writers at Work: The Paris Review Interviews*, p. 246.
17. Ihab Hassan, *Radical Innocence*, p. 131.
18. Ibid.
19. Louise Y. Gossett, *Violence in Recent Southern Fiction* (Durham: Duke University Press, 1965), p. 125.
20. Richard Pearce, *William Styron* (Minneapolis: University of Minnesota Press, 1971), p. 15.
21. Robert H. Fossum. *William Styron: A Critical Essay* (Grand Rapids. Mich.: William B. Erdmans, 1968), p. 10.
22. John W. Aldridge, *In Search of Heresy: American Literature in an Age of Conformity* (New York: McGraw-Hill Book Company, 1956), pp. 146-47.
23. Charlotte Kretzoi, "William Styron: Heritage and Conscience," *Hungarian Studies in English*, No. 5, Debreen, Hungary, 1971.
24. Ihab Hassan, *Radical Innocence*, p. 129.
25. Ibid. p. 132
26. Robert Gorham Davis, "A Grasp of Moral Realities," *American Scholar*, 21 (Winter 1951-1952), p. 116.
27. Jan B. Gordon, p. 110.
28. Jonathan Baumbach, *The Landscape of Nightmare* (New York: New York University Press, 1965), p. 129.

29. David D. Galloway, *The Absurd Hero in American Fiction* (Austin: University of Texas Press, 1974), p. 59.
30. Louis D. Rubin. Jr., "Notes on a Southern Writer in Our Time," in *The Achievement of William Styron*, p. 67.
31. David D. Galloway, p. 61.
32. Marc L. Ratner, *William Styron* (New York: Twayne, 1972), p. 51.
33. W.H. Auden, "The Christian Tragic Hero," *The New York Times Book Review*, 16 December 1945, pp. 1, 21; rpt. in *Moderns on Tragedy*, ed. Lionel Abel (New York: Fawcet Premier Book, 1967), p. 40.
34. W.H. Auden, "The Christian Tragic Hero," *The New York Times Book Review*, 16 December 1945, pp. 1, 21.

3

The Long March

Styron published his short novel *The Long March** immediately after his ambitious first work *Lie Down in Darkness.* This has naturally prompted the critics to view the novella, in comparison with his earlier novel and conclude their analyses of "the extended short story," without adequately discussing in depth the central argument.

The novella has for its theme a thirty-six mile march ordered by Colonel Templeton to strengthen his regiment of marine reservists recalled for service in the Korean War. This creates an absurd situation which Lieutenant Culver helplessly accepts and Captain Mannix violently rejects.

The Long March despite its simple structure, is deft in execution with its taut organisation of several layers of meaning each contributing to the deepening of the central theme: man's violent fight against the almost insurmountable forces in the dehumanized world, and his realisation, in the process, of the sources of compassion.

**The Long March* (London: Hamish Hamilton, 1962). All subsequent references in parantheses are to this edition.

Styron has revealed the autobiographical base of the novel which has dramatized the author's experience in the Marine Corps during World War II as a reserve officer subsequently recalled to active duty in 1950 at the time of Korean War.[1] However, the intense artistic realisation of the experience has transformed it into an extended metaphor of man's predicament in a war-ridden world.

Robert H. Fossum characterizes *The Long March* as "an outcry against the ceaseless war" and goes on to add that its concern is with "a more timeless question" about what man should do when in conflict with those "forces that would not only control his body but break his will, subdue his spirit, and reduce him to robot-like obedience."[2] He believes that Styron has put accent on "the necessity of rebellion in a world without God."[3] He further views the central metaphor of *The Long March* as "that seemingly, senseless and laborious walk through the night"[4] that all men must take until they finally disappear into the universal darkness.

Fossum's reading of the novella is in conformity with his avowed Christian theological predilections. His interpretation of the novel reveals his awareness that violence is the inevitable consequence of man's rebellion in a world which negates his human worth. Yet he would insist that beneath it all, it is a forceful comment on the damage done by "the secularizing of spiritual authority."[5] Although it cannot be denied that *The Long March* is rich in the imagery suggestive of theological overtones, the stress on the final doom of universal darkness would, however, fail to provide the right perspective. Fossum's interpretation, in essence, lays stress on the gloomy aspect leading to universal darkness without taking into account the subtle interplay of compassion with violence, embedded in the novel.

Eugene McNamara also asserts that the novella shows up the Cold War "with its brooding atmosphere of unease and displacement."[6] In his study he points out that the intentional sub-structure of the novel is demonstrated subtly through the plot movement, the narrational mode and the pattern of metaphor. He concludes that all works of art inescapably reflect and echo the tenor of their time achieving their uniqueness through "a certain patterning, a certain cadence of words, a tonal quality."[7] He regards *The Long March* as a work of its time in its revelation that "once we accept the essential absurdity of the modern situation, obedience becomes not only desirable, but imperative" particularly in the context of the inevitable "choice between obedience and destruction."[8] McNamara finds individual rebellion as doomed to disaster and claims that obedience alone would vouch for peace:

> The innocence of childhood is dead, gone. It is replaced by the hard acceptance, by the awareness that we live in a world of irrevocable choices, made even more anguishing and evident by the thermo-nuclear disaster which hovers over him. Peace is a dream. A new kind of peace can be attained through obedience. But the rebellion on an individual level can only mean disaster.[9]

McNamara's view disregards the worth of man's fight in a closed world. Acceptance of "baptism of sweat" need not necessarily lead to a fuller understanding of man's predicament as McNamara seems to believe. Though he takes care to explain that obedience in his interpretation should not be confused with the blind obedience of the Organisation Man, his emphasis on obedience renders the theme of *The Long March* totally pessimistic. In this reading, the violence of rebellion drops out of focus as futile and absurdly comic.

In sharp contrast to McNamara, Peter Hays rightly sets a high premium on the theme of rebellion in *The Long March*. He affirms that works of art do not merely reflect and echo their time as McNamara believes, but they are concerned with the tenor of all time.[10] Since Styron is concerned with the eternal as well as the temporal, the novel, in his opinion, derives its dramatic force from the basic conflict between the stable social order that negates freedom and the rebel who wants to change it all "for the sake of change." The protagonist of *The Long March* in Hays's view, represents "indomitable will in spite of pain and suffering."[11]

August Nigro recognises the necessity of rebellion, even if it be futile as an attempt to assert man's freedom and identity in a society inimical to both. For him the encounter between the hero and the world dramatizes the discrepancy between

American Dream and American Nightmare. Nigro attempts an exhaustive analyses of the novel in terms of its literary allusions, analogues and evocative mythical sub-structure. Nevertheless Nigro appears to be exclusively concerned with "the encounter between the expansive hero and the contained world."[12] He has not, however, explored the violence of the encounter leading to and chastened by the power of compassion towards the end. *The Long March* with its many layers of meaning does not merely dramatise the encounter between the hero and the confined world, but also records the progressive evolution of the protagonist from the elemental violence to the redemptive compassion.

II

The Long March is a piece of documentary fiction in conventional narrative form based on the individual's rebellion against the organised forces of the environment that would compel his surrender. Since the society has accepted the iron frame of system and its mechanistic forces of organisation with inbuilt obedience, it celebrates a remorseless levelling and does not countenance human independence in any form. Every protest and every effort towards identity is ruthlessly put down. As Styron remarks, the story would stress with fierce indignation "that military life corrupts and we would be a lot better off without it."[13] It is a fable of man's rebellion in a world ruled by relentless forces.

The novel opens with the description of a bizarre scene, the irrationality of which shakes up Mannix and Culver:

> One noon, in the blaze of a cloudless Carolina summer, what was left of eight dead boys lay strewn about the landscape, among the poison ivy and the pine needles and loblolly saplings. It was not so much as if they had departed this life but as if, sprayed from a hose, they were only shreds of bone, gut, and dangling tissue to which it would have been impossible ever to impute the quality of life, far less the capacity to relinquish it. (7)

The shocking spectacle on the bright Carolina landscape defines the contrast and provides the starting point of the novella. It underscores the realisation that in peace time there has come suddenly a shell blast to ruin the youth. The sight of death and waste in war time could be ignored "in the same way that a beggar is ignored, or a head-cold or a social problem." (9) but in peace time there is no place for "the slick nude litter of intestine and shattered blue bones." (9) It has descended with deadly impact "like the blow of a fist." The accidental mortar fire which has caused the disaster points to irrational violence erupting suddenly from beneath the calm surface. Mannix and Culver are shocked into the grim awareness of disorder and violence lurking under the cover of smooth system and order. The contrast of order and disorder, of war and peace, and of violence and compassion operates throughout the novel. The irrational violence in peace provokes rebellion. The sight of a faceless youth with "gawky tousled grace" in death outrages Mannix:

> The Captain was sobbing helplessly. He cast an agonised look towards the Colonel, standing across the field, then down again at the boy, then at Culver. 'Won't they ever let us alone, the sons of bitches,' he murmured, weeping. 'Won't they ever let us alone ?' (52)

The rebellious attitude of Mannix is put in proper perspective when it is contrasted with that of Culver. The two reluctant reserves recalled to duty in the Marine Camp find it a dull wasteland. The camp has its tents "on a tiny patch of squashy marshland." (23) Both Culver and Mannix experience a wasteland existence in the camp commended by Colonel Templeton "a man to whom the greatest embarrassment would be a show of emotion." (18) The Colonel who represents the petrified system receives the news of the terrible accident mechanically "as if he were receiving the most routine of messages." (15) This shows up further the dehumanisation at its worst. The feeling is accentuated by the fact that their working hours are spent chasing an enemy who does not exist:

> Not for days but for weeks, it seemed, the battalion had been on the trail of an invisible enemy who always eluded them and kept them pressing on—across swamps and

> blasted fields and past indolent, alien streams. This enemy was labelled Agressor, on maps brightly spattered with arrows and symbolic tanks and guns, but although there was no sign of his aggression he fled them nonetheless and they pushed the sinister chase sending up shells and flares as they went. (32)

Violence permeates the unreal atmosphere of the absurd chase. When free from the farcical chase, they spend their leisure in officer's club ironically called "Heaven's Gate." It renders their very existence lifelessly mechanical and insipid. A deep sense of futility impinges. However, their reaction to this crucial situation marks the separate identities of Mannix and Culver. While Culver reflects, vacillates and finally accepts to a large extent the situation without any violent protest, Mannix rebels furiously to affirm his human worth and he cannot accept his predicament, however helpless and futile his raging against it might prove. Styron presents various reactions to the grim reality in the camp through Culver who observes, experiences and comments illuminating the scene from different points of view.

Looking at the shattered bodies, Culver realizes that the peace time existence with its freedom and serenity in retrospect to have been "a glorious, if somewhat prolonged dream." He remembers nostalgically the vanished simplicity and charm:

> It was one happy and ascending bar that he remembered, a dozen bright notes through which he passed in memory to an earlier, untroubled day at the end of childhood. There, like tumbling flowers against the sunny grass, their motions as nimble as the music itself, two lovely little girls played tennis, called to him voicelessly, as in a dream, and waved their arms. (12)

Culver finds it unusual and inhuman the way Colonel Templeton took the news of the ghastly tragedy and feels convinced that the name "Old Rockey" fitted him most appropriately. When the Colonel orders a thirtysix mile forced march through night as a manoeuvre to strengthen the reserves in *esprit de corps*, Culver has nearly lost his nerve and "began to doze, dreaming fitfully of home, of white cottages, of a summer by the sea. *Long Walk tonight.*" (20) Culver is no doubt a shade better than O'Leary who "had become as inextricably grafted to the system as any piece of flesh surgically laid on to arm or thigh." (22) He dislikes the devoted methodical competence which O'Leary displayed in all infantry jobs he performed. He hates Major Lawrence who practises "third-person flattery" unabashedly with his "baby-blue gaze and parted mouth." But Culver's attitude is typical to the encounter between the Colonel and Captain Mannix when the latter tried to remonstrate against the forced-march on the supposition that most of them in his H & S Company were reserves gone soft for the past few years.

> It was not so much as if he had achieved a triumph but merely equilibrium, had returned once more to that devout, ordered state of communion which the Captain's words had ever so briefly disturbed. At that moment Culver almost liked the Colonel, in some negative way which had nothing to do with affection, but to which 'respect,' though he hated the word, was the nearest approach. (27)

Culver comes close to respect the Colonel, while Mannix darts "a quick look for both fury and suffering, like the tragic Greek mask, or a shackled slave." (28) He feels "suddenly unreal and disoriented." (30)

> . . . adrift at sea in a dazzling, windowless box, ignorant of direction or of any points of the globe, and with no way of telling. What he had had for the last years—wife and child and home—seemed to have existed in the infinite past or, dreamlike again, never at all. . . . All time and space seemed for the moment to be enclosed within the tent, itself unmoored and unhelmed upon a dark and compassless ocean. (31)

Imprisoned in the tent "so much more like a coffin," he realises that the only light in it has "the stark, desperate, manufactured quality of the light one imagines in an execution chamber." (23) The radio signals remind him of "cries of souls in the anguish of hell." He discovers that he is "insecure and uprooted and the prey of many fears." (32)

Condemned to live in "a windowless box" pressed down by an imperious authority and forced to go through the long march which pinpoints the absurdity of existence, Culver and Mannix realise the implacability of blind forces against which there is neither defence nor triumph. Culver reflects:

> Born into a generation of conformists, even Mannix (so Culver sensed) was aware that his gestures were not symbolic, but individual, therefore hopeless, may be even absurd, and that he was trapped like all of them in a predicament which one personal insurrection could, if anything, only make worse. (46)

With the words in parantheses "so Culver sensed" Styron suggests that Mannix's attitude was different. In his helplessness Culver begins to feel "that he had hardly ever known a time in his life when he was not marching or sick with loneliness or afraid." (92) He is convinced that rebellion is hopelessly doomed to failure and therefore futile. He cannot even hate the Colonel because "to hate him would be like hating a cannibal, merely because he gobbled human flesh." (93) It is "a disaster already ordained." He also fears that Mannix in his protest has merely added to "the burden of his vicious fury." Despite his awareness of the futility of the situation, he cannot rebel. He experiences:

> Frustration at the fact that he was not independent enough, nor possessed of enough freewill, was not *man* enough to say, to hell with it and crap out himself: that he was not man enough to disavow all his determination and endurance and suffering, cash in his chips, and by that act flaunt his contempt of the march, the Colonel, the whole bloody Marine Corps. But he was *not* man enough, he knew, far less simply a free man; he was just a marine—as was Mannix, and so many of the other—and they had been marines, it seemed, all their lives, would go on being marines forever; and the frustration implicit in this thought brought him suddenly close to tears. . . .(81)

Culver's understanding of the human situation fails to give him the insight into the necessity of rebellion. He capitulates with the trite compromise that this is after all his lot. A sense of frustration added to the sense of futility confounds him. In this confusion, he cannot appreciate the human dignity of Mannix "because it was simply no longer worth the effort." (88) Culver like the Colonel is of the opinion that "the hike had had nothing to do with courage or sacrifice or suffering, but it was only a task to be performed." (88) He accepts his predicament without a whimper. He stumbles behind the colonel "like a ewe who follows the slaughterhouse ram, dumb and undoubting too panicked by the general chaos to hate its leader, or care." (68) Culver in effect surrenders himself in favour of the routine of life. He is content with success or failure in the conventional ethical mode. He counterfeits his existence as an individual in smug subordination to the social life. He is one of those who think that it is "far easier and safer to be like the others, to become an imitation, a number, a cipher in the crowd."[14]

III

Mannix, a heavy-set Jew from Brooklyn, is also pressed down by the feeling of futility and isolation. He has a disgruntled sense of humour. Recklessly vocal in bitterness, he has profound dislike of the sinister camp life. Although he despises the Marine Corps and its rigid organisation, he finds the whole show as absurdly comic in its irrationality:

> . . . Mannix would laugh. Mannix appreciated the idiocy of those radio words, just as his own crazy way he managed to put his finger on anything which might represent a symbol of their predicament. Like the radio code. He had a violent contempt for the gibberish, the boyscout passwords which replaced ordinary conversation in the military world. To Mannix they were all part of the secret language of a group of morons, morons who had been made irresponsibly and dangerously clever. (37)

Mannix has no illusions about the life in bondage. The sweat, the exertion and the final danger have no charm for him as he is down-to-earth in his assessment and derides "this Hemingway crap." (37) His problem is to get out of the outfit at any rate. He has no wish to be a martyr for some faith. Culver, despite his characteristic detachment, concludes that Mannix was heroic if suffering was part of the hero's role. However, he believes that all heroic gestures were trivial and meaningless as everybody was "caught up by wars in which, decade by half-decade, the combatant served peonage to the telephone and the radar and the thunderjet – a horde of cunningly designed, and therefore often treacherous, machines." (38-39) Valour and honour have no place in a mechanistic content. Mannix's brimming discontent was therefore full of peril. His "persistent, unwhipped, scornful look in his eyes" (42) has no relevance. He disregards his experience of suffering as a victim of mortar fire in the last war. When Mannix pricks the Colonel's sense of importance and pride by refusing to essay "*some kind of an answer*" (43) for some hypothetical and generalised question, he reveals himself "a stubborn and passionate man." (42)

> His words had the quality, the sternness, of an absolute and unequivocal fact, as if they had been some intercession for grace spoken across the heads of a courtroom by a lawyer so quietly convinced of his man's innocence that there was no need for gesticulation or frenzy. (43)

Mannix's anger and hate cannot change anything in the world where everything is fixed with impersonal exactness. When viewed from this background, his rebellion is bound to fail without any impact.

Yet Mannix's rebellion is a studied reaction born of deep awareness of capricious forces operating in the world making of life "a chancy thing" after all. At one stage in the novella, Mannix describes the most horrible experience in his life which brought him close to death:

> We were drunk, you see, polluted, all of us. I think there were five of us, all of us boots just out of Dago. Kids. We were on the tenth floor of this hotel and in this room and I believe we were about as drunk as anyone could get. I

> remember going in to take a shower in the bath room. It was late at night, past midnight, and after I took this shower, you see, I came out into the room buck naked. Two of those drunk guys were waiting for me. They grabbed me and pushed me towards the window. I was so loaded I couldn't battle. Then they pushed me out the window and held me by the heels while I dangled upside-down buck naked in space, ten floors above the street. . . . I got stone-sober in a second. Imagine being that high upside-down in space with two drunks holding on to your heels. I was heavy, man, just like now, you see. All I can remember in those teeny-weeny lights below and the tiny little people like ants down there and those two crazy drunk guys holding on to my wet slippery ankles, laughing like hell and trying to decide whether to let go or not. I just remember the cold wind blowing on my body and that dark, man, infinite darkness all around me, and my ankles beginning to slip out of their hands. I really saw death then, and I think that all I could think of was that I was going to fall and smash myself on that hard, hard street below. That those crazy bastards were going to let me fall. I was praying, I guess. I remember the blood rushing to my brain and my ankles slipping, and that awful strange noise. And I was reaching out, man, clutching at thin air. Then I wondered what that noise was, that high loud noise, and then I realized it was me, screaming at the top of my voice, all over San Francisco. (47-48)

The experience provides a metaphor of the human situation. As Richard Pearce comments perceptively, this reveals "an environment that is urban, military, and dark, man is surprised, ambushed, senselessly assaulted—not to the end of defeat or destruction, not to any end at all."[15] Mannix is a rebel in this wasteland where values are topsy turvy, and the capriciously destructive forces negate man's worth. Styron suggests that the awareness of suffering and the sudden confrontation of death in life has rendered the hairy-chested Mannix more than human:

> he seemed no longer the man who could sicken himself with resentment, but relaxed, pliable even, like a huge hairy

> baby smoothed by the wash of elemental tides, ready to receive anything, all, into that great void in his soul which bitterness and rebellion had briefly left vacant—all—the finality of more suffering, or even death. (49)

Mannix's understanding of life is profound because of his unique experience which has revealed its irrationality. He is detached and unafraid. He begins to question the meaning of existence, and the questioning is informed by deep compassion born of a tragic sense of life. Culver is a stranger to this experience. Loneliness, homesickness and fright alone are the things that count. He fails to assess the resentment of Mannix and feels lost "in terror clutching at the substanceless night."

Mannix's fury makes him a "tormented beast in the cul-de-sac." (51) He cannot compromise with the wanton destruction of innocence. He sobs helplessly looking at the young shell-shattered boy lying there in the blood with his tearful dark eyes as though "he had cried himself to sleep." The spectacle provokes Mannix to spite the system. He accepts the challenge of long march imposed by Colonel Templeton. While Culver accepts the Colonel, Mannix despises him because he represents the dehumanised system which has perfected the organised device that robs him of his freedom.

> He detested Templeton not because of any slight or injustice, but because Templeton was a lieutenant colonel, because he was a regular, and because he possessed over Mannix—after six years of freedom—an absolute and unquestioned authority. Mannix would have hated any battalion commander, had he the benignity of Santa Claus. . . .(19)

Mannix's nightmarish experience at the hotel in San Francisco, the sudden shell blast in the Marine Camp and the meaningless forced march through night confirm his belief that life is at the mercy of irrational forces. His decision to do the forced march in spite of his bitterness is in its nature Sisyphian with a difference. Camus leaves Sisyphus at the base of the mountain 'happy' and he no longer rebels. Mannix's situation is doubtless Sisyphian, but he rebels in order to vindicate that his protest is the only sign of his humanity. Styron enlarges Mannix's personal deprivation into the social context making pointed references to the wrecked Negro cabin:

> . . . shell-shattered doors and sagging walls, blasted facade—a target across which for one split second in the fantastic noon there seemed to crawl the ghosts of the bereaved and the departed, mourning wraiths come back to reclaim from the ruins some hot scent of honeysuckle, smell of cooking, murmurous noise of bees. (51)

The cabin stands as a symbol of ruined peace and the consequent universal deracination. Mannix, the jew, witnesses the shattered Negro cabin. Styron hints at the two most highly persecuted races in human history, and he develops the theme further in the climax.

Mannix goes through the march. In the meantime a nail-end in his shoe penetrates the lining at the base of the heel peeling off a flake of skin and leaving raw nerves exposed. He goads his H & S Company like a galley master to make the march successfully. In his spite of the system, Mannix seems to inherit ironically its values in violently driving his men. He rejects Colonel's offer of truck to get back from the march. He refuses to crap out. Squatting in the sand, Colonel gently strokes Mannix's foot. The "nakedly human" act, in the context of the absurd march ordered by the Colonel himself lacerates the Captain:

> 'Well,' he said, 'may be you'd better ride in on one of the trucks. . .'
> Mannix drew his foot away abruptly, as if the Colonel's hand were acid, or fire.
> 'No. Sir. I'll make this frigging march.' Furiously, he began to put on his shoe. The Colonel rose to his feet, hooked his thumbs in his belt and gazed carelessly down.
> 'I think you are going to regret it,' he said, 'with that foot of yours.'
> The Captain got up, limping off towards his company, over his retreating shoulder shot back a short, clipped burst of words at the Colonel—whose eyeballs rolled white with astonishment when he heard them—and thereby joined the battle.
> 'Who cares what you think,' he said. (72)

In his furious rejection, Mannix becomes guilty of insubordination. The nail wounds him and it may probably bring him tetanus. In any case he is certain to face court martial. Exhausted totally at the end of the forced march Mannix hobbles down the hallway towards the water cooler "naked except for a towel around his waist." (94)

> He was hairy and enormous and as he inched his way towards the shower room, clawing at the wall for support, his face with its clenched eyes and taut, drawn-down mouth was one of tortured and gigantic suffering. The swelling at his ankle was the size of a grape fruit, an ugly blue, and this leg he dragged behind him, a dead weight no longer capable of motion. (94)

Mannix was loath to admit his pain to Colonel Templeton. The Colonel cannot "perform with grace a human act" (71) as he is conditioned by the system and totally dehumanised. The contrast between the inhuman system and the human agent is vividly brought out in the encounter between the Colonel and Mannix. The admission of pain by the Captain is submission to Colonel Templeton. The refusal is therefore celebrated as an essentially human protest. The stubborn captain who discountenanced the Colonel even on pain of court martial sheds his pride before a Negro maid who enquires whether the lacerated ankle hurt him. The Jew and the Negro confront each other. The two understand each other because they have suffered irrational violence and violation of human dignity down the ages. They have endured and they have lasted. They have achieved the perfect understanding of suffering and compassion having passed through the crucible of violence. The human grace and compassion missing throughout in all his other encounters, come with sudden revelation to Mannix in his meeting face to face the Negro maid at the end of the novella. This is the moment of recognition. The look of human sympathy triumphing over the forces of torture vindicates inexhaustible springs of compassion not blighted by the historic violence. Compassion is the balm to the gaping wounds left by the meaningless violence. Styron brings the representatives of human suffering together towards the climax:

> . . . the two of them communicating across that chasm one unspoken moment of sympathy and understanding before the woman, spectacled, bandannaed, said again, 'Deed it does,' and before, almost at precisely the same instant the towel slipped away slowly from Mannix's waist and fell with a soft flop to the floor; Mannix then, standing there, weaving dizzily and clutching for support at the wall, a mass of scars and naked as the day he emerged from his mother's womb, save for the soap which he held feebly in one hand. He seemed to have neither the strength nor the ability to lean down and retrieve the towel and so he merely stood there huge and naked in the slanting dusty light and blinked and sent towards the women, finally, a sour, apologetic smile, his words uttered, it seemed to Culver, not with self-pity but only with the tone of a man who, having endured and lasted, was too weary to tell her anything but what was true.
>
> 'Dead it does,' he said. (94-95)

The juxtaposition of Mannix and the Negro maid is part of the suggestive strategy. Styron reveals at the start the irrationality of the senseless waste of life. It is accentuated by Mannix's horrible experience with the drunks who held him dangling high above ten floors. He then introduces the sudden glimpse of a blasted Negro cabin while the march was in progress. The three scenes unveil the demonic forces acting on life capriciously causing human misery both limitless and purposeless. In the final scene the Jew and the Negro victims of irrational hatred and prejudice stand out as symbols of endurance and compassion.

Mannix's stance is both tragic and human. Styron has hinted through adroit juxtaposition the safe and sheltered world which is blissfully ignorant of the tragic reality. The hero who rebels is ignored, as the world moves on unconcerned, lost in its somnambulistic march. While the hike was in progress:

> A car passed them—a slick convertible bound for the North, New York perhaps—wherever inevitably, for some civillian pleasure—and its fleet, almost soundless passage brought, along with the red pinponit of its vanishing trail lights, a

> new sensation of unreality to the night; the march: dozing, shrouded by the dark, its people seemed unaware of the shadowy walkers, had sped unceasingly on, like ocean voyagers oblivious of all those fishy struggles below them in the night, submarine and fathomless. (67)

The car symbolizes the insensitive world which has no use for the deep and fathomless heroic struggles. All human actions become absurd and meaningless. There is a sense of complete frustration in Culver's realisation:

> How stupid to think they had ever made their own philosophy: it was as puny as a house of straw, and at this moment—by the noise in their brains of those words, *you will*—it was being blasted to the winds like dust. They were as helpless as children. (57)

The world recognises rigid regimentation and moves insensitively rendering all individual human actions trivial and hopeless. Mannix's personal rebellion could only make his predicament worse. His efforts are human and his failure tragic.

IV

The rebellion of Mannix is implicitly tragic because the system against which he rebels seems to leave its impact on the rebel in a pernicious way. Mannix asserts his will and evokes in the reader sympathy for the dignity for the dignity of his stance. But his rebellion is inseparably mixed with his fury as a driving master of his men. He rebels against Colonel Templeton and yet becomes himself despotic like the Colonel to his own men. His rebellion becomes paradoxical. If he did not compel by force his company to make the march successfully he would have failed to spite the system on its own terms. On the contrary, to accept the terms of the challenge transforms him into the force against which he rebels. The inescapable ambiguity of his situation makes his predicament pitifully tragic. Nigro remarks:

> On the one hand, the Corps instills and augments the very pride that moves Mannix to rebellion, and yet it also pro-

> vides the bondage and humiliation which force Mannix to rebel and become that against which he rebels.[16]

Nigro's view that every rebellion is at the source infected is quite perceptive. It renders human situation all the more tragic. But he interprets the motivating forces of human rebellion in Greek terms and regards the pride and will that move Mannix to rebellion as tragic flaws. He calls Mannix's defeat a self-inflicted one. He comments on the identification of Mannix with Achilles by the wound in his heel as "the physical correlative to his more significant internal flaw—his passionate hubris."[17] This imposes severe limits on the meaning of the fable as a whole. Viewed in this light, Gossett's charge that "the violence and the anguish of the rebellion seem nothing more than the imagined reflex of an amputated limb"[18] appears to be plausible.

It should, however, be added that these interpretations go against the weight of metaphoric structure in the work. The concept of *hubris* has to be understood in its true spirit. All pride is not to be confused with the Greek sin of *hubris*. The sinfulness and destructive force are only part of the truth. The Greeks were in fact aware of its immense potentialities in imparting dignity to the rebel. Richard Sewall writes:

> the Greeks respected pride and made it a heroic quality, though they saw its destructive side. Stripped of its eschatology, the Christian doctrine of *felix culpa*, the fortunate fall of Adam, is akin to the treatment in tragedy of the hero's initial crime or sin. Precarious as such an ethic is, tragedy holds aloof from moral judgement and presents the action. in such a way that moral judgement can be only one element, and not the most important, in the total response.[19]

Richard Sewall further writes that "Tragic pride is not to be equated with sin or weakness."[20] Arthur Miller speaks of it as the hero's "inherent unwillingness to remain passive in the face of what he conceives to be a challenge to his dignity, his image of his rightful status."[21] This alone transfigures the common man and makes him a fit subject for tragic treatment. Nigro's interpretation of Mannix's pride deprives him of his tragic dignity and makes him a sinful clown with his unavailing pride. Gossett also accepts Nigro's view and writes off rebellion as a futile attempt:

> in the twentieth century loss of beief in the power of the individual makes the protesting person an anachronism. Violence which might once have had meaning as the attempt of man to justify himself is now an absurd expenditure of energy and nereve. . . . Mannix is aware that his gestures are hopeless because they are individual rather than symbolic. . . . To make a genuine rebellion Mannix needed to be strong enough to care nothing of the false pride of completing the march, for in finishing the hike he and Culver accepted the values of the system they wished to defeat. The fundamental defeat is the fact that the institution has so shaped Mannix and Culver that they cannot effectively will to escape from it.[22]

The argument goes against the very grain of the novella. Mannix's refusal to complete the march would not have revealed the tragic proportions of his individual rebellion against the mighty system. It would have been a suicidal submission to the Juggernaut of authoritarian forces. Mannix accepted the challenge and spited the system in its framework. The foredoomed defeat cannot mitigate the glory of the rebellion. Styron has carefully structured the fable to reveal the essential humanity of Mannix. If the rebellion was absurd, it was by the same token all the more tragic. Robert Fossum comments:

> Mannix's defiance is both hopeless and absurd, his proud endurance is futile in the face of a foreordained defeat. . . . To drop out would be . . . absolute negation, renunciation as well as refusal. Mannix's will to resist, an assertion of the value of his personal existence, makes him *more* than a Marine; it makes him a man who, as Jerry Bryant has said 'imposes human meaning upon that which is surrender and despair would be meaningless.'[23]

Mannix's defiance imposes meaning on the irrational situation. He has endured and vindicated his human worth. As Fossum rightly obsereves that "to endure is to defeat the inhuman machine."[24] The value of "rebellion in reverse" (59) is purely psychological. The rebellion is an inescapable human need as Camus observes that "Man is the only creature who refuses to be what he is."[25] Man's rebellion, Camus further emphasizes, is necessary because

> . . . in every act of rebellion, the man concerned experienced not only a feeling of revulsion at the infringement of his rights but also a complete and spontaneous loyalty to certain aspects of himself. Thus he implicitly brings into play a standard of values so far from being false that he is willing to preserve them at all costs.[26]

Mannix struggles to preserve the value he has cherished: his human worth. He vindicates his spontaneous loyalty by his protest. He rebels as he is inspired by his compassion for the young marines blasted by the mortar. He suffers because of his essential humanity. His failure exemplifies Styron's tragic humanistic stance.

V

The Long March has carefully framed analogues which bring to mind Faulkner's *The Bear* and Melville's *Billy Budd.* Styron explicitly refers to Mannix as "old great soft scarred bear of a man." (85) He is also a "tormented beast in the cul-de-sac," (51) with the "baffled fury of some great bear concerned, bloody and torn by a foe whose tactics were no braver than his own, but simply more cunning." (77) In the final scene Mannix is represented as "clawing at the wall for support." The analogy leads one to Old Ben in *The Bear*. In Faulkner's novella, Old Ben is the wilderness, the mystery of human nature governed by the forms of civilization. The import of the story is that if man succeeds in establishing proper relationship with the wilderness, it reveals to him liberty, courage, pride and humility. The bear in the story is looked upon as a link between man as a rational being and man as a physical creature involved in the mysterious nature. The encroachment of civilization destroys Old Ben, Mannix of *The Long March*, innately free and human is put down by a ruthless system which fails to evaluate his pride, born of compassion.

Mannix is a Christ figure. He invokes Christ repeatedly, and acts out crucifixion hobbling along pierced by a nail, and clutching the wall in agony, naked except for a towel around his waist. He is referred as "Christ on a crutch." (61) The Christian imagery surrounding Mannix, and the religious metaphors characterising the office of the priest-like Templeton put *The Long March* and *The Billy Budd* in sharp contrast. Captain Vere condemns Billy Budd and repents the loss of innocence in the iron frame of legality. Colonel Templeton, on the contrary, has no such awareness. He represents the society that crushes Mannix the individual with blind and insensitive force. In the dehumanised society, the only source of compassion is the sympathetic awareness of suffering. The Negro maid with her awareness of suffering succeeds, whlle "Old Rockey" Templeton fails to get Mannix to confess his pain.

Mannix is called "Atlas like." (65) His dislike of "Heaven's Gate" and his confinement to it out of necessity would reveal him figuratively as being Satanic. Mannix's concern to lead his men successfully through the march as dust rose behind them "like Egypt's pillar of cloud"(79) likens him to Moses. There is rich reference to a cluster of heroes in its quiet descriptive comments on Mannix.

Styron has put Mannix in the line of heroic tradition on purpose. It shows up the violent struggle between the hero and the narrow confines within which he acts. Styron reveals his deep meditation on human situation by this juxtaposition. Nigro makes a perceptive study of the analogies but his conclusion puts Mannix in an unfavourable light:

> This evocation of traditional heroes works contrapuntally and the reader feels the heroic dimensions of Mannix's act, but also the sharp incogruity between their grand defeats and Mannix's ignoble defeat—between Achilles' powerful lament and vengeance for the death of patroclus, Atlas staggering labour beneath the pillars of heaven, Prometheus's ordeal on the rock of ages, Satan's titanic fall from heaven to hell, Adam's temptation and fortunate fall, Mose's struggle in the exodus from Egypt, Christ's passion and resurrection,

> Ahab's magnificent failure to destroy the white whale between all these and Mannix's paralysed, spastic, hobbling entrance into the camp.[27]

To regard the mythic parallels as a device to reveal the incongruity is to ignore the force of tradition altogether. The act of rebellion itself has made all ages contemporary. The fate of all the heroes cited, has been uniformly tragic. Styron's emphasis is on the tragic sense of life and its dignity born of integrity. Nigro himself recognises "the basic integrity and nobility of the stance."[28] He calls it an "indictment of the meek, willless masses who give up their freedom without even a whimper."[29] The hero rebels against the system which destroys compassion and tenderness. The value of the protest is what matters, regardless of victory or failure. Ratner aptly comments that "rebellion even in its failure is preferable to Faulkner's or Hemingway's stoic endurance."[30] This aspect is very important in the evaluation of *The Long March*. It documents the struggle of the protagonist to retain his integrity as a subjective value. This is his definition. Commenting on *The Long March*, Styron has said:

> My story's hero is also a rebellious soul, a young Marine reserve officer whose mutinous rage against authority in general, and his commanding officer in particular, leads to his downfall. . . . He resists the system and it is his ruin. You cannot buck the system—I think that is what I was trying to say—for if you do, you will pull disaster down upon your head.[31]

However, Styron does not intend any extraordinary simplification in total disregard of the symbolic and mythological density reflected in the novella. He adds: "Divorced of its philosophical content the narrative becomes utterly routine."[32] Styron is aware that the protagonist is in line with the rebel tradition of literature and mythology in the Western civilization. Mannix should be interpreted as a rebel in the light of Camus' definition of the positive aspect of the value implicit in every act of rebellion, as the rebel "is fighting for the integrity of one part of his being."[33]

Mannix's remonstration against what he considered a futile and senseless violent regimentation in the very nature of things took the form of a defiant obedience to the system of which he was a part. Neverthless there is a pronounced streak of rebellion even in this conformism. In order to expose the insanity implicit in this ruthless and almost sadistic command of Templeton and its dehumanizing effect, he (Mannix) valiantly takes up the challenge of the long march, and spurns assistance offered by Templeton, even when he bled profusely because of the piercing shoe nail. He was content with his self-pride to the point of obduracy rather than submit to the bogus benevolence of a military dictator.

It is only when the Negro maid expressed her anguish—which struck him with the resonance of a true voice of feeling—that he involuntarily responded with "Deed it does," that he is able to regain his compassion which is the essence of humanity and justice.

Mannix's suppressed anger is against the system which made him just a cog in the infernal war machine; a robot and a moron to carry out and execute orders from above which lacked reason, imagination and humanity. He would never abdicate his right to be human and so his courageous march should be seen as a unique indictment of the closed system which outrages human values. Styron has made the implication further clear:

> . . . I began to understand, as I wrote, that even in the midst of an ultimate process of dehumanization the human spirit cannot be utterly denied or downed: against all odds, faces emerge from the faceless aggregate of ciphers, and in the middle of the march I was creating I found Captain Mannix slogging and sweating away, tortured, beaten, but indomitable. A hero in spite of himself or me, he endures, and in the midst of humanity retains all that which makes it worthwhile to be human. I myself cannot be sure, but possibly it is the hopeful implications derived from this mystery—this kind of indefatiguable man—which are all an artist can pretend to suggest, however, imperfectly, in his

struggle to comprehend the agony of our violent, suicidal century.[34]

Mannix's rebellion is born of compassion. His profound shock at the shell-shattered youth, and his impatience with the system which would not recognise human element had made him the rebel he was. His raging against the system generates violence which brings about suffering. Mannix comes to realise the springs of compassion through suffering. Styron has emphasized this by bringing face to face the representatives of long suffering in human history. Violence and suffering have vindicated the integrity of the protagonist.

Violence in *The Long March* has led the protagonist to the sources of compassion. The dialectic of violence, suffering and compassion is examined in greater depth in *Set This House on Fire*.

NOTES

1. James L. W. West III, "William Styron's Afterword to *The Long March*," *Mississippi Quarterly*, 28, No. 2 (Spring 1975), p. 187.
2. Robert H. Fossum, *William Styron: A Critical Study* (Grand Rapids, Mich.: William B. Erdmans, 1968), p. 20.
3. Ibid.
4. Ibid.
5. Ibid.
6. Eugene McNamara, "William Styron's *Long March*: Absurdity and Authority, *Western Humanities Review*, 15, No. 3 (Summer 1961), p. 267.
7. Ibid.
8. Ibid., p. 270.
9. Ibid., p. 272.

10. Peter L. Hays, "The Nature of Rebellion in *The Long* March," *Critique*, 8 (Winter 1965-66), p. 73.

11. Ibid., p. 74.

12. August Nigro, "*The Long March*: The Expansive Hero in a closed world," *Critique*, 9, No. 3 (1967), p. 107.

13. William Styron, "If You Write for Television," *New Republic*, 146 (6 April 1959), p. 16.

14. Soren Kierkegaard, *The Sickness Unto Death*, trans. Walter Lowrie (Princeton, N.J.: Princeton Univ. Press, 1941), p. 51.

15. Richard Pearce, *William Styron* (Minneapolis: Univ. of Minnesota Press, 1971), p. 20.

16. August Nigro, p. 105.

17. Ibid., p. 110.

18. Louise Y. Gossett, *Violence in Recent Southern Fiction* (Durham, N.C.: Duke Univ. Press, 1965), p. 121.

19. Richard Sewall, *The Vision of Tragedy* (New Haven and London: Yale Univ. Press, 1970), p. 62.

20. Ibid.

21. Arthur Miller, "Introduction to *The Collected Plays*" in *Arthur Miller's Collected Plays* (New Delhi: Allied, 1973), pp. 3-35.

22. Gossett, p. 121.

23. Robert Fossum, p. 23.

24. Ibid., p. 24.

25. Albert Camus, *The Rebel* (London: Hamish Hamilton, 1960), p. 17.

26. Ibid., pp. 19-20.

27. August Nigro, pp. 111-12.

28. Ibid., p. 112.

29. Ibid.
30. Marc L. Ratner, "Styron's Rebel," *American Quarterly*, 21, No. 3 (Fall 1969), pp. 596-608.
31. William Styron, "If You Write for Television," p. 16.
32. Ibid.
33. Camus, *The Rebel*, p. 23.
34. James L.W. West III, "William Styron's Afterword to *The Long March*", pp. 188-89.

4

Set This House On Fire

Styron's third novel *Set This House on Fire** is voluminous and episodic in sharp contrast to its predecessor *The Long March.* Its complex structure has led many critics to misconstrue the novel as a vainly ambitious effort. In the first few months of its publication *Set This House on Fire* was subjected to bitter criticism, almost to the point of vituperation, accusing Styron of celebrating crude violence without artistic justification for the many outrageous themes in it. While Marvin Mudrick has dismissed it "as full of cardboard wolves with grinning teeth,"[1] *Virginia Quarterly Review* has found in it a mere conglomeration of "the assorted horrors so bountifully displayed" and questioned whether it was artistically necessary to represent in such detail the scenes of "seduction, rape and murder and general depravity." The reviewer has finally concluded that "there is no discernible allegory, no symbolism worth mentioning; and there is no study of evil as a force contesting for the soul of a man." The novel for him merely

---

**Set This House on Fire* (London: Jonathan Cape, 1970). All subsequent references in parantheses are to this edition.

reveals that a great deal of talent is wasted on such tawdry material.[2] In a brief write-up *Times Literary Supplement* finds the form of the novel inadequate for Styron's grotesque and luxuriant talent.[3] Phoebe Adams, however, shows some insight when she discovers the fact that *Set This House on Fire* is essentially religious in intention," but considers it a defect to record every step of the progress of Cass Kinsolving from darkness to light.[4] Even a perceptive critic like Arthur Mizener who admires Styron's skill and sophistication describes the characters of the novel as "the stock figures of romantic melodrama."[5]

The sort of adverse criticism is due to the fact that *Set This House on Fire* is cast in a mould that goes beyond the beaten track of recent fiction, and thematically probes into the nature of good and evil in the regeneration of spirit from utter degradation, through violence and suffering. The impatience with the theme of the novel, explains much of the criticism that goes off tangentially.

Styron has deliberately exploited almost all the technical and thematic nuances of the Western tradition, as he brings into the novel the aspects of parable, fable, allegory and symbolism along with the burden of eschatological questions. The symbolism of *Set This House on Fire* is an important factor on its interpretation. The inability to evaluate its symbolic pattern would make the action grossly inflated. Symbols from the Book of Revelation and also a good deal of apocalyptic material abound in the novel. The complexity, both structural and thematic, has prompted Ratner to comment that

> Styron provides enough symbolism and myth to satisfy the formalists, he sufficiently discusses the malaise of American Society to appeal to sociologists and European critics; he suggests the influence of Camus and possibly Kierkegaard to interest existentialists.[6]

All these different factors do not, however, fall apart. It should be said to Styron's credit that the novel has made use of all these various elements to project the theme of salvation through suffering that exemplifies modern human condition. It is an attempt to exploit the traditional modes of thought and technique to the fullest extent while being averse to the traditional dogmas. Styron has succeeded in making the protagonist of the novel "ordinary yet capable of tragic passion, contemporary yet aware of the literary past, a pathetic victim yet striving for freedom to act."[7] These paradoxes and contradictions of "a rending conflict within a man" resolve themselves in the structural pattern of the novel. Styron realises the sources of tragic vision when he wrestles in his novel with the questions of fate, freedom and responsibility. He tries to touch the core of Christianity in his analysis of sin and redemption through love. In his awareness of the force of Nietzsche's famous dictum that "God is dead," he probes into the meaning of life coming very close to the existentialist tradition. In his emphasis on Faith, he throws light on the inner chaos of man.

The religious experience evoked in the novel springs from the protagonist's "encounter with the deepest and most encompassing elements of life in which he has found meaning."[8] The search for meaning involves destructive violence in various forms as the victim is forced to resort to murder in order to create. The element of violence in *Set This House on Fire* becomes a means to discover the springs of compassion in man's life which is essentially tragic.

The tragic plot is worked out in the novel on various levels. Styron has explicitly brought it very close to the spirit of Greek tragedy. Against this background *Set This House on Fire* reveals itself as a novel of violence leading to man's redemption from sin, through suffering and compassion. The allegorical, symbolic and episodic movements of the narration tend to heighten the tragic sense of life in the explication of its meaning. The possibility of tragedy in modern times lies in man's agonising search for values, however ordinary and commonplace his life may be. The tragic sense is independent of the rank and magnitude of status. Arthur Miller has this to say on the tragic predicament of man while explaining his own concept in his plays:

> There is no doubt that if a character is shown on the stage who goes through the most ordinary actions, and is suddenly revealed to be the President of the United States, his actions immediately assume a much greater magnitude, and pose the possibilities of much greater meaning, than if he is the corner grocer. But at the same time, his stature as a hero is not so utterly dependent upon his rank that the corner grocer cannot outdistance him as a tragic figure—providing of course, that the grocer's career engages the issues of, for instance, the survival of the race, the relationships of man to God—the questions, in short, whose answers define humanity and the right way to live so that the world is a home, instead of a battle ground or a fog in which disembodied spirits pass each other in an endless twilight.[9]

The questions whose answers have direct bearing on the definition of humanity, spring from man's confrontation with the fact of existence. The Aristotelian concept of stature is inapplicable in the evaluation of tragedy. Arthur Miller further argues:

> the lasting appeal of tragedy is due to our need to face the fact of death in order to strengthen ourselves for life, and that over and above this function of the tragic viewpoint there are and will be a great number of formal variations which no single definition will ever embrace.[10]

This reading helps us evaluate Styron's perspective correctly. The understanding in depth of life and death constitutes tragic vision. Violence in tragedy, when tempered by compassion, creates meaning in the protagonist's life that seems fortuitous till the moment of crisis. The recent American novel has thus come to be "a twisted manifestation of the spirit" with its necessary insistence on violence and tragic vision. This may be due to the kinship with Baudelairian notion that "the only way to pray in the modern world is to blaspheme, the only way to live is to hurt, the only way to act is to remain passive."[11] The way to affirmation through negation and void has given the recent fiction a mode which Ihab Hassan explains as the "deflection of spirit" from traditional forms or goals and believes that the deflection in the contemporary novel reveals "the underside of consciousness, where all true tests are faced, and out again, beyond the crisis of nihilism which is the primary threat of our time."[12] As a counter to nihilism Camus proposes the Sisyphian happiness. The existential stance of Sisyphus is to discover grounds for living in life itself when this life appears to be drained of its meaning.[13] In literature the pattern adopted to illustrate the Sisyphian affirmation includes violence, since the lucidity of existence is realised only in the context of violence. In recognition of this fact Hassan announces that "the spiritual baptism of our age is a baptism by tar."[14]

Styron explores "the underside of consciousness" through his allegiance to the existentialist mode of literature bristling with violence that leads to compassion as a redeeming factor. He seems to favour "thematics" rather than formalistic aesthetic in uncovering the tragic vision in its original Dionysian spirit without the imposition of Apollonian restraint. The violent pattern is further relevant as the genuine tragic vision could be understood *in extremis* alone. Murray Krieger writes:

> The tragic vision, a product of crisis and of shock is an expression of man only in an extreme situation, never in a normal or routine one. Literature dealing with it frequently dwells on the exceptional man; and when it does choose a normal man it does so only to convert him, by way of the extremity he lives through, into the exceptional man. The tragic vision is . . . a vision of extreme cases, a distillate of the rebellion, the godliness which, once induced by crisis, purifies itself by rejecting all palliatives. And the tragic visionary . . . is the extremist who . . . finds himself transformed from character to fable.[15]

The extreme situation transforms a normal man into an exceptional one to reveal the sources of tragedy. This is the mode of indirection the post-war novelists have preferred through fable, allegory and symbol. Styron adopts the mode for *Set This House on Fire* to record Cass Kinsolving's spiritual metamorphosis through violence and suffering. Unfolding its meaning on various planes, the novel becomes by turns a

Greek tragedy, an existential novel, a fable of violence, a Christian allegory of redemption, and a parable of suffering and compassion.

II

Styron sets the tone of the novel with a crucial passage at the very outset recording an angry old man's fulminations against the nation of smugly contented soap peddlers.

> "What this great land of ours needs is something to happen to it. Something ferocious and tragic like what happened to Jericho or the cities of the plain—something terrible I mean, son, so that when the people have been through hellfire and crucible, and have suffered agony enough and grief they'll be men again, human beings, not a bunch of smug contented hogs rooting at the trough. Ciphers without mind or soul or heart. . . ." (15)

The need of tragedy of the dimensions of the Old Testament suggests the technique of the novel as well. The furious apocalypse with its allegorical significance develops gradually culminating in the protagonist's choice of being. *Set This House on Fire* has three points of view in its narration which Styron appears to have adopted after his conscious experiment with several factors of fictional technique in *Lie Down in Darkness* and *The Long March*. Peter Leverett, the narrator and also Jamesian central intelligence is introduced very blandly in the beginning:

> My name is Peter Leverett. I am white, Protestant, Anglo-Saxon, Virginia-bred, just past thirty, in good health, tolerable enough looking though possessing no romantic glint or cast, given to orderly habits, more than commonly inquisitive. . . . (4)

The ordinariness of the narrator brings out the formal and thematic unity of the novel. The whole novel divided into two parts—one narrated by Peter and the other supplemented and filled in by Cass—will impart fullness to the unravelling of the mystery of what happened in Sambuco and its purpose. Styron has put "ordinary" narrator to temper the turbulence of the extraordinary events relating to the existentialist hero acting out in an extreme situation of horrid violence. Though Abraham Rothberg considers that Peter could be dispensed with as a narrator without much harm to the novel, one feels that the detached view of Peter is, however, very important to act as a foil to the compulsive involvement of the protagonist.[16] He is integral to the structure and can be done away with only at the expense of the formal design very much germane to the theme.

Set This House on Fire has planted itself squarely in the contemporary history to render its theme of spiritual redemption credible. Styron compels our attention to the incongruous social problem—the agonising gap between the extravagant riches and pitiful poverty—dramatizing the situation in the presence of an opulent American Film Company against the background of war-ravaged and poverty-stricken Italy. The social purpose is unambiguously revealed when a character is made to comment:

> Some day the Russians will have the refrigerators and the bathrooms that you Americans have. But though it is repressed at the moment, the Russians have a fund of spirituality which you Americans have never developed. They will be educated people with refrigerators and bathrooms. You will be ignorant people with refrigerators and bathrooms, and the educated people will triumph. (354)

Although spirituality is the prime concern of the novel, human depravity is examined and commented upon from various perspectives to drive home the need of tough tragic understanding of the worth of life. The absence of tradition and spirituality nourishing the past haunts American mind in its quest for anchorage. Peter says:

> Perhaps one of the reasons we Americans are so exceptionally nervous and driven is that our past is effaced almost

> before it is made present; in our search for old avatars to contemplate we find only ghosts, whispers, shadows: almost nothing remains for us to feel or see, or to absorb our longing. (18)

America is therefore "the land where the soul gets poisoned out of pure ugliness." (283) Cass also despises the easy going Northerners who never can understand the problem of the South and yet prescribe easy recipes suavely "because we know it's good for you, and it's humane, and it's decent and American." (369) Since Cass comes from the South "a guilt-burdened region," his life becomes a desperate struggle to find deliverance from evil which haunts him in several forms. The apparent social and political criticism is employed to project the tragic view of all history as "error, dream and madness." (464) Styron is concerned with broadening of the theme of guilt and judgement along with the theme of redemption beyond despair. The endeavour entails structural complexity as Styron includes social criticism in order to clarify the terms of his protagonist's transcendence.

Transcendence of despair in the novel is enacted in a violent context involving three Americans: Peter Leverett, Cass Kinsolving and Mason Flagg. The story has a twenty year time span, relates to two continents and the whole modern history. Cass Kinsolving, the protagonist, acts out in his life the tense drama of spiritual redemption through violence, suffering and compassion.

Styron prefaces his novel with a long quotation from John Donne's sermon "to the Earle of Carlile, and his company, at Sion" and borrows the title of the novel from the agonising passage:

> .... that God, who, when he could not get into me, by standing, and knocking, by his ordinary means of entering, by his Word, his mercies, hath applied his judgements, and shaked the house, this body, with agues and palsies, and set this house on fire, with fevers and calentures, and frighted the Master of the house, my soule, with horrors, and heavy apprehensions, and so made an entrance into me. ...

Cass is the anguished man of the novel who wrestles with God and with himself realising his "foulest uncleanness" and shakes the house of his body with agues and sets it on fire. Cass's struggle parallels in its sheer helplessness another crucial passage from the sermon:

> . . . what gnashing is not a comfort, what gnawing of worme is not a tickling, what torment is not a marriage bed to this damnation, to be secluded eternally, eternally, eternally from the sight of God ?

The acute feeling that he is barred from fulfilment in his life plagues Cass and he reaches the depths of depravity. A series of violent events dredges him out from the infernal agony and puts him on the road of discovery. *Set This House on Fire* documents the fall and redemption in a violent way suggested by the Donne passage prefacing it.

The story is narrated through a disconnected series of reminiscing conversations, letters and diary notings. The strangely muted and contorted style of the novel reflects the chaos within. Though Virginia is in the background of the novel the violent action takes place, in the main, in the village of Sambuco, Italy. Cass has gone there with his family to rediscover his strength as an artist. In his expatriate poverty and in his total surrender to alcohol he becomes a victim of Mason's devilish pranks and plays the obscene buffoon. Peter Leverett finds Cass in this abject state when he arrives in Sambuco as Mason's guest. He stays on to witness a series of violent events that form the staple of the novel: a rape, a horrifying death and a murder.

Leverett realises that the chaotic disorder has dated from the day he left Rome for Sambuco on invitation from his malignant, wealthy and flamboyant friend Mason Flagg. Driving through the suburbs of Naples he samshes a motor scooter. The one-eyed Italian, Luciano di Lieto with a long history of accidents, falls unconscious and Leverett takes the responsibility to pay the hospital bills. Suffering from extreme nervous exhaustion he reaches Sambuco in a badly damaged car. The series of incidents starting on a near comic tone gather momentum swiftly to reach the crescendo of total horror. He later in the day comes in contact with Cass's family and also the American movie crew on location in Italy making an extravagant film based on a costume novel. He learns the utter humiliation of Cass in bondage to Mason Flagg. He comes to know the role of the beautiful Italian girl Francesca in Cass's life. In the end he is shocked by the mysterious murder of Flagg. The experience of Sambuco somehow gets deeply planted in his mind and he is tortured by dreams of treachery and betrayal:

> Who had betrayed me ? Whom had I betrayed ? I did not know, but I was sure that it all had something to do with Sambuco. And although I felt little grief over Mason's end—I want to make that clear right now—I still felt low, miserably low over what had happened in that Italian town. Now, looking back on it, I can see that maybe it was only because my most unhappy suspicion was this: that though I was in no way the cause of Mason's death, I might have been in a position to prevent it. (6)

Several years after the Sambucan tragedy, Peter drives to Charleston South Carolina to meet Cass who "had his own private riddles to solve and untangle." (51) And just as Peter thought that he could clear up his oppressive mysteries, he also discovers that Cass saw in him the key to his own. Peter is the detached participant in the story "like some private seeing eye." He remains, as Galloway points out "the only uncorrupted male character in the book."[17]

Peter explicates Mason's past as the story moves on. Through his love-hate relationship with Mason, he reveals that the debased American from the North has not changed much from the days at St. Andrews into whose pious Christian precincts he had "burst like some debauched cheer in the midst of worship." (73) Mason can get to know his identity only through others. Displaying his wealth, he seduces people to entertain him at the expense of their individuality. His flamboyant speeches on the death of art and importance of sex are cheap and overblown and are calculated to win the attention of others. A coward by nature, he invents fake stories of his adventure, based on others's experiences. Posing as a creative artist and ill-treating the women under his control he reveals his shallow and anti-humanistic self. His indecently publicised sexual activity becomes a means to express his individuality through rape, both figurative in the case of Cass and literal in the case of Francesca. While reminiscing, years after Mason's death, Cass tells Peter:

> All the time I spent with Mason, I felt I never knew him, never could put my hands on him. He was like a gorgeous silver fish in a still pond: make a grab for him, and he has slithered away, and there you are with a handful of water. . . . He was like mercury. Smoke. Wind. It was as if he was hardly a man at all, but a creature from a different race who has taken on the disguise of a man, . . . For him there was no history, or, if there was, it began on the day he was born. Before that there was nothing, and out of that nothing sprang this creature, committed to nothingness because of the nothingness that informed all time before and after the hour of his birth. And it was impossible to understand a creature like this. . . . (446)

Mason is the negation of all that is human and totally indifferent to the meaning of life born of responsibility and struggle for freedom. Instead of confronting his own self, he is chiefly concerned with others depriving them of their essential human worth. He symbolises the dark void that engulfs life.

Cass Kinsolving is in the centre of the novel. Styron's delineation of the predicament of Cass has prompted Robert Gorham Davis to call the novel "more or less existential."[18] John Howard Lawson[19] and Ihab Hassan[20] have agreed on its pervasive existential frame. Lewis Lawson has analysed Cass brilliantly as a "Kierkegaardian man of despair."[21] There is no denying that there are a great many symbolic and even patently verbal references to Kierkegaard throughout the novel. It should, however, be noted that Styron has made use of this modern philosophy as part of his strategy to vividly portray the contemporary tragedy. It was not his intention to present a fictional commentary on Kierkegaard's *Sickness Unto Death*. The exclusive insistence on the existential element limits the scope of the novel. Though the conflict between Mason Flagg and Cass Kinsolving defines the pattern of action in the novel, its chief element lies in Cass Kinsolving's spiritual crisis. The psychological element is more important because of the inner conflict which Cass has to face squarely and set himself free through violence "as the violence is a necessary preliminary to Self-discovery and redemption."[22] Cass realises the need of violence as he begins to confront his own depravity which has led to his captivity. He is very much aware of the lack of freedom in the aimlessness of his life in Europe where he is trapped by terror, booze and Mason, the symbol of corruption. Nevertheless Cass has enough integrity to realise that he alone is to blame for his failure. He tells Peter:

> How can you ever know where the blame lies ? What part was Mason's and what part was mine and what part was God's. I've had nightmares about it—or I used to, before I got hold of myself—and in these nightmares someone or something told me that it wasn't Mason who was the culprit—wasn't Mason who was the wicked party—but only by your friend the preacher here, who was the evilest man who ever walked. (248)

Cass's struggle with God begins very early. He is the orphan of an Anglican minister brought up by a Methodist uncle. Though an Episcopalian of sorts, he has married poppy, a devout simple Catholic. He returns from the war abandoning religious faith. He struggles with himself and yearns for "some kind of woolly and comforting darkness." (54)

Cass's confronation with darkness within, has its source in his failure to capture the divine spirit that has gone out of him. In its absence he feels put down by the burden of guilt and realises in great anguish that his soul is on sinking sand. The loss of divine spirit is connected with two episodes. The first of them is the vision he experiences in Paris when he drunkenly wanders in his apartment, his steps leading him to a window overlooking the city:

> and I'll swear at the moment as I looked up it was as if I were gazing into the kingdom of heaven. I don't know quite how to describe it—this *bone-breaking* moment of loveliness. . . . It was as if I had been given for an instant the capacity to understand not just beauty itself by its outward signs, but the other—the elseness of beauty, this continuity of beauty in the scheme of all life which triumphs even to the point of taking in sordidness and shabbiness and ugliness, which goes on and on, and of which this was only a moment, I guess, divinely crystalized. . . . And it filled me with the craziest sort of joy. . . . (256-57)

He connects the joy born of this Manichean vision with his youthful seduction of Vernelle Satterfield. She refers to his orgasm as loss of the divine spirit: "Why the divine spirit just flowed right on out of you." (265) Cass accepts her comment as significant. His search for the divine spirit is also linked with his sense of guilt and undiscoverable crime. He has spent his insecure boyhood in the south. He is a psychotic discharged uncured from a Navy hospital. He remembers the tortured days of World War II. He recalls his conversation with the psychiatrist who has presented him with a two volume edition of Greek drama. He has told Cass, "you will be running all your life." (314) The search has begun quite early and also the sense of guilt. Cass traces the source of his guilt to his experience as a boy working in a Western Auto store deep in the back country of Virginia. His friend Lonnie took him out to dispossess a radio from a Negro farmer who had failed to keep up with his payments. In their search they found the cheap plastic radio and then destroyed the cabin as an act of sheer vandalism. Cass remembers:

> I knew it was wrong, I knew it, I knew it—bestial, horrible abominable . . . but it was as if once I'd lost my courage anyway. . . . I could actually do what I was doing almost even with a sense of righteousness. All the cliches and shibboleths I'd been brought up with came rolling back—a nigger wasn't much more than an animal

anyway, specially field niggers, crooked niggers like this Crawfoot. . . . (377-78)

This memory exercises strong unconscious pressures on Cass. He keeps dreaming of Negroes. The guilt and shame smother him. Cass has thus a long way to go. His search is two-fold. He has to find the divine spirit that has fled from him. He has to exercise the guilt within him. This brings into focus the symbolic significance of Michele and Francesca in the novel. The thraldom of Cass under Mason also adds meaning to the symbolic context. The proper evaluation of the role of many apparently disconnected incidents and characters thus becomes necessary to understand the fulness of Cass's redemption through violence. It is evident that Cass Kinsolving's world had lost its meaningful centre the moment he came in contact with Mason and tasted the first bottle of whisky that hurled him into the abominable servitude. He lates tells Peter:

> I got so that with Mason I was as helpless as Romulus, sucking on the fat fit of a wolf. But this day there, this day he gave me that bottle, I had no idea how far *in* I would get with Mason, how deep and involved. Any more than I had the notion that in another way I'd rouse myself—God knows how I did it—and grasp a truth about the shabby and contorted life I'd been leading and make at least a stab at salvaging something out of the wreckage. . . . (402)

The salvaging of the wreckage or the redemptive possibility is realised through his friendship with Francesca, the beautiful peasant girl. He finds in her "a kind of serenity and repose that I never really knew existed." (440) He goes with her into the valley where she was born. He has begun to try hard to save Michele her tubercular father. He makes use of his bondage to Mason to fetch medicines for the dying poor peasant. The compassionate endeavour becomes a firm basis for his redemption. As Mason tries to make his ownership of Cass complete, he realises that Francesca is the one area in the life of Cass that remains uncovered. He is keen to violate this area and deprive Cass of all possibility of perspective or focus. Towards the end Cass learns with the wisdom of hind-sight that his abject surrender to Mason contained within it the seeds of redemption. He confesses:

> And the paradox is that this slavish contact with Mason that I had to preserve in order to save Michele freed me to come into that knowledge of selflessness I had thirsted for like a dying man, and into a state where such a thing as dependence on the likes of Mason would be unheard-of, an impossibility. And Mason must have understood this, too, and not so dimly either. . . but that I still remained, each hour I strove to bring Michele back to health . . . . I moved closer to a condition of freedom, and Mason knew it even if I didn't and this he couldn't bear. (443-44)

Mason tightens his grip over Cass by keeping the pills which Cass needs for Michele. His compassionate commitment to Michele has given Cass something to live for. Cass gets to understand that his failure to possess life has deprived him of the ability to give life to the dying peasant:

> Mozart gives, he thought, giving more in one sweet singing cry than all the politicians since Caesar. A child gives, a shell or a weed that looks like a flower. Michele will die because I have not given . . . hell is not giving. (453)

The compassion he feels for Michele has, however, set him free from the guilt he has experienced as a Southerner over the plight of Negroes and especially the guilt born of his direct involvement in the destruction of Negro Crawfoot's cabin. While attending on Michele in his dirty hut, Cass suddenly connects Michele with Crawfoot:

> . . . then he had inhaled deeply, almost relishing the sour and repellent smell, then almost choking on it as

> he filled his lungs with the thick putrescent air, in a hungry effort to dislodge from memory that moment in years forgotten when he had smelled this evil smell before, when suddenly he knew, and thought: It is niggers. The same thing by God. It is the smell of a black sharecropper's cabin in Sussex County, Virginia. (416)

The service to Michele has brought Cass closer to "a condition of freedom." (444) While Michele is associated with the guilt over Negroes, Francesca symbolizes the divine spirit that has fled from Cass. When Cass is sure to possess the *joy* in her, Mason rapes Francesca as a punishment for an alleged theft. The rape of Francesca is not merely a physical violation for Cass; it becomes a spiritual abomination, a negation of all that is pure and divine. Cass rages as he tells Peter:

> . . . by raping her he raped the two of us: that night I felt he had committed some filthy, unspeakable violation upon life itself. His timing was perfect. At that very moment when through Francesca I had conceived of life as having some vestige of a meaning, he tore that meaning from limb to limb. (444)

Cass's search for meaning finds near-fulfilment in his compassion for Michele and Francesca. Its violent negation by Mason compels Cass to murder him as he believes that Mason was not only guilty of rape but also of killing Francesca. Cass in his rage bashes Mason's skull with a stone and heaves the body into the void from a mountain peak. The only overt act he has committed in order to affirm order and values has been ironically an agonising moral wrong. Although Mason raped Francesca, he did not kill her. As she was running away from Mason in fright, the village idiot Saverio approached her. He got frightened by her frenzied attempts to escape from his harmless caresses, and mutilated her violently, oblivious of the act he was committing. Francesca, the symbol of innocence, beauty and purity is raped and murdered violently and gratuitously. Subsequently Cass learns that Mason is not guilty of her murder, he loathes himself profoundly for the moral wrong, and decides to commit suicide. Luigi, the intellectual Italian policeman who has earlier befriended Cass comes to his rescue, alters the evidence relating to Mason's murder and leaves Cass free. He urges Cass to realise the good in himself, and not to "sin in this guilt of yours." (490) Luigi has earned a profound understanding of life in the bitter experience of tragedy. He recounts the terrible bombing by the allies:

> . . . just as my brother ran into the vacant lot a British plane came over and dropped a bomb . . . . I looked into the lot and I saw my little brother running towards me, clothed in flame. He was *on fire* ! He ran toward me all ablaze, screaming in a way that I never knew a child to scream. It seemed the whole city were filled with the sound of his screams. It was like *angels* screaming: And then he fell to the street in front of me, blazing like a torch. He died right away. He was no more than a blackened little cinder. I wept. (494-95)

The memory of his little brother has haunted him and deprived him of faith in "a God who could create a universe in which it would be possible for a single innocent child to suffer like that." (495) He remembers that he wept once again only when he found a crumpled note of hope in the hands of an English woman who spent all her days in lonely spiteful misery and always "demanded much and gave nothing." (495) For the third time in his life he wept when Francesca died. He tells Cass:

> It was not for you that I wept, not for Francesca, but without self-pity for myself—because I understood something. When I wept in this extraordinary way, which is so rare for me, I could not help but think again of my brother and the English woman and then all that had happened there in Sambuco, and I wept out of my own understanding. And that understanding was that this existence itself

> is an imprisonment. Like that English woman we are serving our sentences in solitary confinement, unable to speak. All of us. Once we were at last able to take with our Jailer, but now even He has gone away, leaving us alone with the knowledge of insufferable loss. Like that woman, we can only leave notes to Him—unread notes, notes that mean nothing. I do not know why this has happened, but it has happened, that is our condition. In the meantime we do what we can. (497)

Luigi has suffered enough violence, and nihilistic despair agony. The compassion born of this deep insight into life brings him to advise Cass "to enjoy whatever there is left in life to enjoy." (499)

Cass experiences Cathartic grief, as he thinks of Francesca, Michele and Mason. He becomes past all misery and rage. He goes back home to America. In the end Cass tells Peter:

> '. . . I wish I could tell you that I had found some belief, some rock, and that here on this rock anything might prevail—that here madness might become reason, and grief joy, and no yes. And even death itself death no longer, but a resurrection.
>
> 'But to be truthful, you see, I can only tell you this: that as for being and nothingness, the one thing I did know was that to choose between them was simply to choose being, not for the sake of being, or even the love of being, much less the desire to be forever—but in the hope of being what I could be for a time. This would be an ecstasy. . . ." (500-01)

Cass's comment appears towards the end of the novel. With this he closes the episode of violence and his escape from the impending prison through the help of Luigi. In sharp contrast to the agonisingly ruffled events, the narration takes place while Cass and Peter are on a fishing expedition. He speaks of the events as a detached observer:

> '. . . I thought of Francesca and Michele, and all that I had lost, and the grief came back in a wave, then it went away.

> 'I thought of Mason, too, but nothing happened. . . .' (499)

He comes back to his wife, children and America:

> now in this morning light I heard the children call out to each other, and I could see them playing some game which was more like a dance. I didn't know what it was but there they were sort of strutting face to face and soundlessly clapping their hands together, like some vision of Papageno and Papagena, or something even more sweet, paradisaic, as if they were children not really of this earth but of some other, delectable morning before time and history. I watched them as if I were watching them for the first time in my life, or as in a dream. (500)

The vision reveals to Cass the force of the statement "learn to enjoy whatever there is left in life to enjoy." (499) He realises the continuity and serenity of life through the innocent purity of children as if in a vision. He has come to affirm life after having been through the darkest phases of it. He has known the gruesome consequences of gratuitous violence. He has assessed the impact of monstrous global violence through the episode of innocent child (Luigi's brother) dying of burns. Once he has come to the conclusion that life prevails despite violence, he knows that it is man's lot to cherish the few glimpses of innocence, beauty and purity. Cass has learned this, and therefore remembers quietly the import of Luigi's comment "Because if by now, through what you have endured, you have not learned *something*, then five years, ten years, fifty years in jail will teach you nothing.'" (499) Thus Cass has come to choose "being" finally.

Cass has come to choose "Being" finally as he has gone through violence and discovered "the joy within" and redemption through compassion. In the end, he can serenely review the tragedy as he has vanquished his former self through the experience of violence, suffering and compassion.

III

Depravity, drunkenness and soulless slavishness have kept Cass down till he has come to realize *something* out there by the redemptive role of his association with Francesca. The evolution of Cass is further evident in the way he reacts after the murder of Mason Flagg. Cass had no knowledge of guilt when he destroyed the Negro cabin. The sense of guilt comes as Cass touches the springs of compassion in his regeneration through a violent process. The act of murder becomes a means to discover compassion. At the moment of killing Mason, Cass realises the impact of violation in the spiritual regeneration as he suddenly feels that the murder has imperilled the humanistic order.

> *Children* ! he thought, standing erect over the twitching body. *Children* ! *My christ* ! *All of us* !
>
> Then in his last grief and rage he wrestled Mason's body to the parapet, and wearily heaved it up in his arms and kept it for a moment close to his breast. And then he hurled it into the void. (464-65)

Cass reaches the end of the road after the murder of Flagg. He comes to choose "Being" and affirms it in one of the two letters fixed at the end of the novel "who was it in Lear who said ripeness is all. I forget, but he was right." (506) The other letter is equally suggestive of the redemption. Peter gets it from a nurse of the hospital where Luciano di Lieto has been undergoing treatment. She informs him that he has made an amazing recovery from the state of coma in which he has been languishing for many months. He has risen like "the phoenix risen from the ashes of his own affliction." (506) She comments that "the durability of this young man is truly remarkable," and adds that Luciano is affianced.

The symbolic role of Luciano, and Saverio has to be understood in full to get at the underlying significance of the novel as a parable of regeneration through violence and compassion. Richard Pearce regards the Luciano story as a comic frame for the serious theme of regeneration.[23] Luciano's engagement parallels the blissful reconciliation of Cass to his family. Pearce also finds that Saverio is Luciano's tragic double whose murder of Francesca is an amoral act.[24] Saverio appears last in the novel "babbling happily and didn't seem to have any knowledge or recollection of what he had done." (493) The symbolic importance of Luciano appears to be as suggestive as the affirmative painting of Harry in *Lie Down in Darkness.* The Rabbi in the painting seems to hold forth some hope for the world which has become void of sense. In the final analysis however it is merely a painting and fails to correspond realistically to the world situation. In the same terms Luciano has come out of his suffering gleefully like the phoenix, but his portrayal is much too weak to add substance to the allegorical framework in a convincing way.

Saverio, however, is weighty in the symbolic framework of the novel. He kills without motive and unconsciously. His act is simply gratuitous and amoral. He represents the violence that erupts from beneath irrationally as "surprise, ambush and accident." The irrational violence of the world is a force which cannot be either foreseen or controlled. It lies underneath the very smooth structure of the society. That life is hemmed in and threatened by the irrational forces of violence symbolically is pointed out in the character of Saverio. The easy optimism stands questioned, mocked and negated by the violence of surprise.

Cass has not made an easy choice in the end. He is fully conscious of the basically tragic character of human life. Very early in his reminiscences he has told Peter that he has never had faith in God "some dis-embodied gaseous vertebrate." (294) His life has become a search for meaning and the agonising search is revealed through his nightmares and dreams. His nightmares, always associated with Negroes, have found a final exorcism in the Michele episode. He connects the poor Italian peasant with the Negroes in their tragic existence. The death of Michele has revealed to him the horror of poverty and the tragedy of existence. The other dream which is described at considerable length in the novel concerns an old woman with a heavy load of faggots which she cannot heave up. The burden is too great for her emanciated body. He later dreams of travelling a Pullman which has suddenly run over a dog. It is brutally crushed with its hinder parts right up to its chest smashed flat. The poor beast gives a heart breaking whimper and tries with his forepaws to raise itself from the earth. The driver of the bus gets down and keeps thrashing away at his skull hoping to free the dog from the torture. The dream continues:

> It was not now the dog's head he was beating, but the head of the woman, this scrawny peasant woman the faggots. Somehow she had turned into the dog. Lying there crushed and mangled, with her poor tormented body pressed against the dust, she let out piteous cries, shrieking, 'God ! God !' over and over again. 'Release me from this misery' And each time she called out, *down* would come the flailing stick which would knock her bleeding head against the earth, only for the head to rise again to cry out for deliverance from all this agony, and each time again the stick would strike her, futilely, releasing her not into death but only into an endless mystery of pain. (357-58)

The dream compounds many fragments of tragic experience and seems to emphasize that life is tragic as it has no saving grace. God appears to have created suffering mortal flesh as a capricious error. The suffering is all the grimmer as even God cannot deliver the creatures from pain. A compassionate gesture turns out to be cruel and tragic. The peasant woman's indescribable misery is doubled by the only human gesture—the torture by the failing stick. The irrational and unspeakable suffering underlying the world perverts the act of compassion into a harsh chastisement.

Cass's quest for redemptive salvation has gone on a tortuous route. He has gone through darkness, nothingness, suicide and thoughts of homicide. The journey further leads him to the vision of unsullied innocence, goodness and beauty. Francesca symbolizes this vision which has the force to set him free from the coils of nefarious evil. Cass is inspired to affirm "Being" through the act of violence to shatter Mason the embodiment of the evil like stomping "a flea carrying bubonic plague, getting rid of the disease and the carrier all at once." (129)

The violation of Francesca reveals to him the enormity of evil. His awareness of the tragedy is acute as it juxtaposes the gruesome rape and murder of Francesca with his experience of "this momentary, fabulous and bountiful peace" (440) in the secluded grove where she poses for him in the nude. The beatific vision is necessarily momentary because it is too pure and good for this world. The absolute 'transcendal purity can come but as a flash. The experience of the vision forces on him the fact that he has to confront darkness and evil on the road to salvation. The village half-wit Saverio, the devilish Mason, the dissipation of Cass and the violation of Francesca are the various forms of violence which have a definite function to perform in the story. Commenting on the pervasive violence as the tragic fact of existence, Pearce remarks:

> the novel has a powerful effect, aud the effect results from the disconnections. Cass is haunted by expressions of violence that are not congruent with mental and physical surfaces. . . . And beneath the surface that Americans have created to disguise life also lie the violence of possessiveness, expressed in Mason's manipulation of Cass, the violence of arrogance, expressed by the movie company taking over Sambuco, the violence of class division, expressed in the life of the peasant woman with her mountain of faggots, the violence of laissez-faire individualism, expressed in the rape of Francesca, the violence of carelessness expressed by the bus driver running over the dog.[25]

These many forms of violence are brought into focus by the culminating fact that the murder of Francesca was an accident. The experience of random violence stares in the face and it gives a sudden jerk to the carefully planned story of the novel, at once manifesting the disconnectedness of events and Cass's quest for redemption. The redemption of Cass is a challenge to "a kind of sleazy common prostration of the human spirit." (116) Styron illustrates the process of redemption by various means—symbolically through Saverio and Francesca, allegorically through Mason and Cass.

The novel demands a comprehensive view of all the elements forming the final structure to project Cass as *everyman* of modern tragedy. As Urang observes *Set This House on Fire* becomes a story of potentially tragic involvements as we begin to appreciate and identify with Cass Kinsolving "with his zest for life, his capacity for love, his creative impulses, his curiosity and intelligence."[26] We get an insight into the suffering that characterizes Cass's life as we evaluate his journey in the modern Wasteland with his self-pity, terror and rage.

Galloway defines Cass as a tragic hero who affirms moral cause and effect in spite of its cruelty. Styron fully appreciates the classical tragic vision. He has very subtly structured his novel with unmistakable suggestions to the Greek tragedy. He keeps the tragic world of Greek tragedy in the background of one's consciousness while evaluating modern human tragedy in its various forms. It is not done with a view to forcing the usual incongruity in providing the parallels. Styron emphasizes the fact of tragic vision as the essential truth of life. Galloway comments on the strong parallels the novel has with the Greek tragedy:

> The tragedy that takes place in Sambuco first comes to Leverett through a series of wailing cries similar to those which might be made by the chorus in a Greek play. The first words of explanation which he hears are 'Quelle horreur ! . . . Quelle tragedie.' (219) Pressed for more details, the money-conscious hotel owner, Windgasser, can only mutter, 'Overpowering twagedy, my God. It's like the *Gweeks*, I tell you but far worse !' Describing the crowded square into which he runs, Leverett notes that 'A squad of carabinieri entered in a riot truck, stage right,' (221) and when the horrifying events of the day are over, Cass comments to Leverett, '*Exeunt Omnes*. Exit the whole lousy bunch.' (239) Thus, as seen through Leverett's eyes, the tragedy which occurs in Sambuco observes the unities of the time, place and action; it constitutes, in fact, a kind of play within the novel.[27]

The presence of the classical tragedy suggests that easy and optimistic redemption is out of place in man's life. In addition,

Cass quotes *Oedipus at Colonus* several times in the novel. Working out the Greek parallels in detail. Moore remarks that Styron is "not subtle about these literary parallels" and complains that he is "mechanically and academically soaking up influences.[28] There is hardly any doubt that Styron would have us "keep the Greeks always in mind." Styron goes to the Greek tragedy as he realises that modern human condition needs a Cathartic experience. Cass rants out at one stage:

> We'll bring back tragedy to the land of the Pepsi-Cola and the peanut brittle and the Modess Because . . . *Tragedy* by God, that's what will give 'em ! Something to stiffen their spines and firm up their joints and clean out their tiny little souls. (118-19)

The presence of the design of Greek tragedy and also the references at the start of the novel to what happened to Jericho, are intended to explicate the truth that has characterised human life in all times and all places. It also lights up what lies underneath the Hebraic, Hellenic and Christian traditions. Styron has very skillfully contrived the orchestration of the three elements to enlarge and deepen the tragic sense of life. Cass is made in the image of Oedipus, and he experiences fulfilment of the Book of Revelation in the murder of the Beast—Mason Flagg. He comes very close to realise the redemptive power of Christian grace towards the end. The modern secular world which has its roots in the three great traditions has not confronted the sense of futility and hopelessness in a way independent of the traditional source. Though the experience of life has been uniform throughout human history, the tragedy of modern world is searingly stark as it has failed to respond to the vision born of Faith, Catharsis and Grace. The Hebraic faith has sustained man to love life as "Somehow, all things do work together for good; in other words, the practical religious solution is a deep hope turned into an adventurous faith that the power of God is matched by his infinite goodness."[29] But modern man's dilemma lies unresolved as he has lost faith in God. The Greeks have recognised "an unalterable cosmic framework" and also realized the absence of purpose in human life. Yet they have given expression to their love of life "in terms of truth, beauty, and goodness."[30] This double vision of life has produced the Greek sense of tragedy. They have looked upon suffering and pain as a Cathartic (purificatory) act to confront the ambiguity of existence. Since the man in the modern world has lost all sense of comic framework, his suffering and struggle fail to achieve the cathartic function. The Christian Grace is beyond him "since there is thought to be no God who judges one guilty and is capable of offering forgiveness and reconciliation."[31] Walter Lippman writes with emphasis that although modern man has abandoned his faith in the religious story of the Christian Gospel "he has not ceased to be credulous and the need to believe haunts him."[32] Styron is hinting at the need to win Grace in the modern predicament and he appears to be close to Unamuno's tragic sense of life in bringing Cass to the verge of nullity and despair through violence and agony. Cass's realisation parallels Unamuno's belief that man must experience despair, doubt and agony in order to reach the solid "foundation upon which the heart's despair must build up its hope,"[33] and it should ultimately become "a basis for action and morals."

Urang is of the view that Styron has made the Biblical images and allusions more pointed and functional than the few passages of existentialist language. He believes that the texture of the novel leads one to realise in Christian terms the power which is inseparable from the recognition and acceptance of a forgiving and restoring work of "grace."[34] Analyzing the novel in terms of Tillich's "Courage to Be," Detweiler concludes that Cass has, in his choice of Being, truly had religious experience, as the power to accept being is the power of grace itself. He calls it genuinely religious though not grounded on the formulas of dogma.[35] The choice of "Being" towards the end led the critics to interpret the novel variously in the light of Hellenic, Hebraic, Christian and existential terms. However, Styron seems to insist that human life is basically tragic. It is full of violence which surprises and overwhelms all order and pattern. Violence inevitable leads to suffering. Man discovers the meaning of existence through suffering which acts as a force to release the springs of compassion. The affirmation of being is reverence of life. The discovery of compassion, through violence asserts the view that man's search for meaning is not easy to come by. In its commitment to "the courage to be" the search may appear to be "rooted in the God who appears when God has disappeared." Styron has chosen to express it in a very guarded and tentative way. Cass Kinsolving does not assert that he has experienced the power of "Grace," but nevertheless he reveals the tragic intensity of his search for meaning in the world that negates it.

The novel has therefore concluded on a very ambiguous note. Yet, it has, through its complex episodic form, driven home the tragic fact of redemption by violence and compassion.

The dialectic of violence and compassion gains articulation with greater clarity in Styron's last novel to date *The Confessions of Nat Turner* which he has chosen to describe as his "meditation on history."

NOTES

1. Marvin Mudrick, "Mailer and Styron: Guests of the Establishment," *Hudson Review*, 17 (Autumn 1964), p. 366.
2. *Virginina Quarterly Review*, 36, No. 4 (Autumn 1960), pp. civ-cv.
3. *Times Literary Supplement*, 17 February 1961, p. 101.
4. Phoebe Adams, *Atlantic Monthly*, 206 (July 1960), pp. 97-98.
5. Arthur Mizener, "Some People of Our Time, "*New York Times Book Review*, 5 June 1960, p. 5.
6. Marc L. Ratner, *William Styron* (New York: Twayne, 1972), p. 70.
7. Gunnar Urang, "The Voices of Tragedy in the Novels of William Styron," in Nathan A. Scott, Jr., ed. *Adversity Grace: Studies in Recent American Literature* (New York: Frederick Ungar, 1960), p. 202.
8. Robert Detweiler, "William Styron and the Courage to Be," *Four Spiritual Crises in Mid-Century American Fiction* (Gainesville: University of Florida Press, 1964), p. 13.

9. Arthur Miller, "Introduction," *Arthur Miller's Collected Plays*, (New Delhi: Allied Publishers, 1973), p. 32.
10. Ibid., p. 33.
11. Ihab Hassan, "The Way Down and Out," *Virginia Quarterly Review*, 39, No. 1 (Winter 1963), p. 81.
12. Ibid.
13. R.W.B. Lewis, *The Picaresque Saint* (Philadelphia: 1959), p. 17.
14. Ihab Hassan, "The Way Down and Out," p. 83.
15. Murray Krieger, *The Tragic Vision* (Chicago: The University of Chicago Press, 1966), p. 20.
16. Abraham Rothberg, "Styron's Appointment in Sambuco," *New Leader*, 43 (4-11 July 1960), p. 26.
17. David D. Galloway, *The Absurd Hero in American Fiction* (Austin and London: University of Texas Press, 1974), p. 67.
18. Robert Gorham Davis, "Styron and the Students," *Critique*, 3 (Summer 1960), p. 44.
19. John Howard Lawson, "Styron: Darkness and Fire in the Modern Novel," *Mainstream*, 13 (October 1960), p. 17.
20. Ihab Hassan, "The Character of Post-War Fiction in America," *English Journal*, 51 (January 1962), p. 7.
21. Lewis Lawson, "Cass Kinsolving Kierkegaardian Man of Despair," *Wisconsin Studies in Contemporary Literature*, 3, No. 3 (Fall 1962), pp. 54-66.
22. Marc L. Ratner, "Styron's Rebel", *American Quarterly*, 21, No. 3 (Fall 1969), pp. 596-608.
23. Richard Pearce, *William Styron* (Minneapolis: The University of Minnesota, 1971), p. 28.
24. Ibid.
25. Ibid., p. 34.
26. Gunnar Urang, p. 206.
27. David D. Galloway, pp. 77-78.
28. Hugh L. Moore, "Robert Penn Warren, William Styron, and the Use of Greek Myth," *Critique*, 9 (1967), pp. 103-12.
29. J. Calvin Keene et.al , *The Western Heritage of Faith and Reason* (New York: Harper and Row, 1963), p. 126,

30. Ibid., p. 210.
31. Ibid., p. 657.
32. Walter Lippmann, *A Preface to Morals* (New York: The Macmillian Company, 1929), 8 f.
33. Quoted in *The Encyclopaedia of Philosophy* (New York: The Macmillan Company and The Free Press, 1967), p. 184.
34. Gunnar Urang, p. 200.
35. Robert Detweiler, p. 13.
36. Paul Tillich, *The Courage to Be* (New Haven and London: Yale University Press, 1959), pp. 189-90.

5

The Confessions of Nat Turner

Styron's *The Confessions of Nat Turner** has received wide publicity for several reasons, not all of them strictly concerned with literary evaluation. Since the relationship of the races is considered a chief factor of the novel, "it has provoked and will continue to provoke both thoughtful and extreme reactions."[1] Although initial critical response was favourable, the novel became a subject of serious controversy, as the critics began to view Styron's treatment of the historical facts relating to the life of Nat Turner either from a technical point of view or from a social perspective exclusively. Stanley Kaufmann, for instance, has faulted Styron on picking up Nat's life as a subject for tragedy asserting that "as a revolutionary hero for a work of art . . . he (Nat) simply does not exist."[2] He is further convinced that "as a drama between man and God,"

* *The Confessions of Nat Turner* (London: Jonathan Cape, 1968). All subsequent references in parantheses are to this edition.

the novel has failed and lost "a chance for tragic stature." Alan Holder has commented that Styron has not made the book commensurate with the mighty theme he has chosen. He writes:

> Though he (Styron) has evoked a sense of place, he has not achieved his main task, the creation of a protagonist who compels our belief in him as a probable or even possible Nat Turner. The book moves waveringly among its personal, social, and religious planes, uncertain itself as to where Turner's reality is located.[3]

Wilfrid Sheed is in agreement with Holder, although he feels that "if the book fails by default, as a novel, it does succeed in many places as a kind of historical tone poem."[4] He describes the novel as Styron's "signal, non-literary service" in that it successfully documents the physical situation of slavery.

Richard Gilman states clearly "that literature as literature, has nothing to do with history, other than being able to draw upon it as it is free to draw on anything,"[5] and exempts Styron's novel from the charge that it is not faithful to the historical truth. Yet he concludes that as "fiction with a tragic and religious impulse and ambition" the novel fails to succeed.

The critical antipathy to the novel springs from interpretations that treat it either as a historical novel or as a work of art independent of history. A more useful approach to the novel could perhaps view it as the culmination of Styron's efforts to validate the dynamics of suffering, violence and compassion. He has skilfully made use of the confessional technique to reveal the authenticity of experience which is unique as it unfolds several layers—social, religious and humanistic—converging into a well-structured modern tragedy. The world of *The Confessions of Nat Turner* is action-packed, violent and hopeful. It exemplifies a lonely man's symbolic journey through *Inferno*, *purgatario* to *paradiso*, as Nat experiences the abominable slavery, goes through the bloody bath of rebellion, and finally attains the compassionate understanding of life. Nat is *Everyman*. Styron has attempted to go beyond the confines of Southern background even though he has planted his story in the 19th century Virginia. The *locale* provides a historic base and realistic contours to human tragedy.

While the 19th century Virginia plantation life has the doomed mood of Greek tragedy, the historical facts of Nat's life have made it inevitable for the novelist to exploit the Biblical rhetoric through the moving imagery of the Book of Revelation. The only sustained and significant slave revolt of 1831 becomes a rich fable that emerges from and goes beyond historicity.

Nevertheless the publication of *The Confessions of Nat Turner* in the fall of 1967 triggered off a violent reaction largely because it touched the sensitive nerve of American experience—the racial relationship—particularly in the wake of Negro riots of Detroit and Newark. The mood of anger was not specially suited to judge the novel objectively and Styron has quite understandably been dubbed as a perpetrator of white racist myths and stereotypes. The Negro writers were provoked to issue an angry protest *The Ten Black Writers Respond.*[6] The Black writers potest "that the Nat Turner created by William Styron has little resemblance to the Virginia slave insurrectionist who is a hero to his people."[7] They are convinced that the historical facts relating to real Nat Turner are "far more dramatic than the imaginary scenes created for this novel."[8] The Black critics have complained that "the distortion of the true character of Nat Turner"[9] as intentional, and dubbed the novel as "a dubious literary adventure" of "an unreconstructed Southern racist." The distortions referred to could be summarized thus:

(*i*) Styron has made Nat Turner a celibate with intense longing for white women ignoring the fact that Nat had a wife.

(*ii*) The novelist disapproves of the historical arrangements of the Turner family and diminishes the role of Nat's parents and grandmother in shaping his strong character.

(*iii*) Styron portrays the Negroes as willless Sambos and minimizes the significance of several waves of slave unrest insisting on the uniqueness of the Turner rebellion. Aptheker considers the pattern wrong.[10]

(*iv*) The author has deliberately turned Nat's fellow-rebel Will into a monster while Gray's "Confessions" record him as a remorseless rebel committed to the task of winning freedom at all costs.

(*v*) The novel records that the armed slaves loyal to their masters put down the Nat rebellion most vigorously. Aptheker comments that "Everything here is made up out of whole cloth and is false."[11]

(*vi*) Styron has made Nat into a vacillating Hamlet uncertain of his mission and unable to act just when the insurrection has commenced. This is in sharp contrast to the fact that Nat in prison, helpless, injured and facing execution quietly said, "was not crucified ?" in reply to the court-appointed white lawyer's query if he (Nat) did not see that his entire mission was wrong. This epic grandeur of Nat's character is lost in the novel.

All these constitute "the manipulation of history and of fact" which is deliberate on the part of the author. The motive for this distortion, the Black writers maintain "could be William Styron's reaction to the racial climate that has prevailed in the United States in the last fifteen years."[12]

Such analysis, however correct in point of Nat's historicity and biography, fails to take into account the authenticity of Styron's *The Confessions of Nat Turner* as a work of art. The crucial changes made by the novelist in the life incidents and character of the protagonist may well be disputed, if viewed through the precisionist eyes of a historian or a biographer, but one cannot challenge, in my opinion, the imaginative design of *The Confessions of Nat Turner* where the hero retains an independent integrity and identity in his own right.

Styron has made it clear that *The Confessions of Nat Turner* was historical, social and topical only peripherally. Its real purpose was to explore the mysterious human psyche grappling with the experience of suffering, violence and redemption.[13] It is a fable of man's search for love and joy in a world which accommodates evil in its darkest form. Styron has seen the implications of "a tremendous theme"[14] in the historical Nat Turner's bloody mission to free his fellow slaves.

The historical rebellion of Nergo slaves against their white masters took place under the leadership of *Nat Turner* in the late Summer of 1831, in a remote section of South-Eastern Virginia. The short-lived rebellion though put down immediately took a toll of sixty white people. The rebel salves were arrested, tried and executed. About two hundred innocent Negroes were brutally killed by the whites during the reprisals that followed. Nat Turner, captured on October 30, 1831 was taken the following day to the jail in Jerusalem, county seat of Southampton county. The next day, a white court-appointed lawyer, Thomas R. Gray, eager to know as much as he could about the rebellion, visited Nat Turner in the prison cell and found him ready to talk. Gray recorded Nat's statements and subsequently published a 5000-word pamphlet "The Confessions of Nat Turner," together with a list of the white victims and the Blacks who were charged with participation in the rebellion. By way of introduction, "To the public," he wrote:

> This is a faithful record of his (Nat Turner's) confessions. . . They certainly bear one stamp of truth and sincerity. He makes no attempt (as all the other insurgents who were examined did), to exculpate himself, but frankly acknowledges the full participation in all the guilt of the transaction. He was not only the contriver of the conspiracy, but gave the first blow towards its execution.[15]

This brief transcript is the single most important source of the uprising. It informs us of Nat's early life, his mastery of the Bible, his religious fanaticism, and the reasons which impelled him to rise up against the whites of Southampton county.

In "The Confessions" Nat creates the impression of an extraordinary character. Gray adds that "for natural intelligence and quickness of apprehension he is surpassed by few men I have ever seen."[16] At one stage Nat counters Gray with "was not Christ crucified?" when asked if he did not feel mistaken in his failure. To the end he remains unrepentent forcing his confessor to record:

> The calm and deliberate composure with which he spoke of his late deeds and intentions, the expression of his fiendlike face when excited by his enthusiasm, still bearing the stains of blood of helpless innocence about him; clothed with rags and covered with chains, yet daring to raise his manacled hands to heaven, with a spirit soaring above the attributes of man, I looked on him and my blood curdled in my veins.[17]

In the context of the unique character of Nat Turner and the exceptional nature of his revolt, "The Confessions" throws up certain intriguing facts. First, Nat masterminded the bloody rebellion though he did not personally suffer much since his master was kind to him and placed confidence in him. Second, he found himself unable to kill when the occasion demanded though he had instructed his followers that "neither age nor sex was to be spared." (Always it was Will who intervened and despatched the victim.) Third, Young Nat's only murder was that of Margaret Whitehead—a hapless nubile girl.

These facts have guided Styron in his novel to connect Nat's motivation for violence with the dehumanizing institution of slavery and its inbred psychosexual problems; and to explain Nat's inability to kill in the light of his essential humanity and his compassion.

In Styron's novel the story is narrated by Nat Turner himself. *The Confessions of Nat Turner* begins with the "Judgment day" on which Nat is sentenced to die on the gallows. It then goes back in narration by "Visions, Dreams, Recollections" to the "Old Times Past" of Nat's childhood and youth; it moves on to "Study war" the description of the massacre; and it ends with Nat's execution in "It is Done." Styron has made language a fit medium to express the tangled emotions and to meet the many needs related to a slave's condition. Nat speaks to his White masters in a servile whining dialect, to his fellow slaves in a carefully articulated language of an oppressed people, and to himself and his God in an archaic Biblical language.

Through his creative imagination, Styron has achieved personal identification with his character by narrating the story in the first person. Styron has spoken at length about the significance of the technique:

> I was up on Martha's Vineyard and I had just read for the first time Camus's 'The Stranger.' It is a brilliant book, the best of Camus, and it impressed me enormously; there was something about the poignancy of the condemned man sitting in his jail cell on the day of his execution—the existential predicament of man—that hit me. And so did the use of the first person, the book being told through the eye of the Condemned. The effect of all this was so strong that I suddenly realized that my Nat Turner could be done the same way: that, like Camus, I would center the novel around a man facing his own death in a jail cell, which of course was true of Turner and how his life ended. And so there suddenly provided, was the architecture of the book, its framework, along with the idea of telling the story in the first person.[18]

"The poignancy of the condemned man" and "the existential predicament" provide an insight into the pattern of the novel. Styron is concerned with the basic human element involved in the terrible tragedy that happened in history. He was not in fact interested in the external features of the historical time and place, but it was "a meditation on history" in the sense that he would exploit the historical facts to reveal the themes "that concern the human life and its peculiar emotional gravity in this period and any other – the inner world."[19] Exploring the tragedy that has overtaken a sensitive human being in a particular period, Styron unfolds the tragic aspect of human life transcending time and place and gives "a concrete prehistory of the present."[20] Styron's chief concern is to bring "Nat to life as a complex, deeply human person of tragic dimensions."[21] The other extraneous details and his departures from the text of the original *Confessions* are not really important.

Fidelity to "the outer world" which constitutes the actual events and characters of the particular historical period should be reconstructed imaginatively to reveal the emotional life or what George Lukacs calls "the life of the common people and the way history (as we know it from the vantage point of the present) impinges upon them."[22] Styron reveals the inner life of the era that found justification for the institution of slavery and also the man oppressed by it to the extent that violent rebellion became inevitable. The era in fact made the man. He rebelled not merely because the inhumanity of the institution was intolerable, but because he realised that his humanity could not be stifled with. The misery of his own life and his compassion for the slaves around his came to have a special meaning and bearing in the light of Nat's capacity to observe, meditate and react. Styron has put it as his aim "to recreate a man and his era, and to produce a work that is less an "historical novel" in conventional terms than a meditation on history."[23] He is aware that the man he wanted to recreate was "one of the few slaves in history who achieved identity."[24] The importance of the novel could be grasped better when it is interpreted as a study of the complex human being who was unique and whose history has "a felt relationship with the present."[25] Although the author was content "to tell the truth about what it was to be a slave of a certain sort in early years of the last century"[26] in the context of the slavery which was an abomination and horror, he did not want "to shirk what must have been after all the tolerable aspects of the situation,"[27] since the poised portrayal would uncover its ugliness more poignantly. The uncompromising courage to confront the facts in their totality prompted Styron "to assume the persona of a Negro."[28] Negro symbolizes the dispossessed. He asserts that "if you can sympathize with the dispossessed, you can certainly take on the lineaments of the Negro."[29] The first person narrative was therefore not merely a technique or bold acceptance of a challenge. It was more properly a moral imperative for him. A meticulous observation of Negro—even Faulknerian in its fulness—would be a veiled artistic evasion. He wanted *to think* and *to live* Negro.[30] Once the first person narrative was solved technically, the author took upon himself to get inside the mind and psyche of "the prodigious blackman."[31] The objections raised against the propriety of the technique fail to impress because something more serious than mere technicality is involved—the stature of the protagonist as a man evolving through the condition of his servitude, his spirituality, his religious fanaticism and his psycho-sexual complexity. Styron has thus attempted a complex fable to embody the dynamics of suffering, violence and compassion. The departures from the original "Confessions" and all the inaccuracies that Styron is accused of become meaningful in structuring the fable. The fable calls for interpretation on various levels as it explores the social, religious and personal compulsions of violence.

II

In the first place Styron evokes the institution of slavery in all its grim cruelty. He takes care to show that even the little acts of kindness within the system tend to make it all the more unbearable. The novel reveals that the institution of slavery was a necessary condition for the very existence of the Whites. In all its various modes slavery obliterates the slave's identity. Styron constructs a number of episodes to unravel the mystery of Nat's violence especially in view of the confessed fact that his owner treated him with kindness and placed confidence in him. In his understanding of slavery Nat has gone beyond its personal impact viewing it as the one handiwork of devil and supreme evil. He realises that the inhuman walls that imprison slaves can never become tolerable whatever be the temporary remissions in the form of little acts of kindness. Styron very ingeniously reveals Nat's psychological wound that lies retching as he contemplates the plight of Negro children that come into his view as he looks through the jail window:

> As always there were four of them, four black children; the oldest could not have been older than eight, the smallest was younger than three. Dressed in shapeless clothing which some troubled mammy had fashioned for them out

of cotton sacking or the poorest odds and ends, they picked their way along beneath the trees on the far bank, gathering twigs and fallen branches for some cabin fireplace. Pausing, stooping down, suddenly scampering forward, they moved with quick and sprightly motions beneath the clumsy flapping of their formless little sacks, piling twigs and sticks and faggots high in their arms against their bodies. I heard them call out each other. I couldn't make out their words, but on the cold air their voices were shrill and bright. Black hands and feet and faces, bobbing, swooping, dancing shapes silhouetted like lively birds against the white purity of the forest and the morning. I watched them for a long time as they moved, all unknowing, doomed and hopeless, across the clean space of snow and finally vanished with their burdens, still sweetly chattering and shrill, upriver past the limit of my sight.

Suddenly, I thrust my face into my hands, thinking of Daniel's beast again in the burning visions of the night, thinking of Daniel's cry: *O my Lord, what shall be the end of these things ?* (40)

The description is highly ironical. The poor black children are like lively birds quick and bright. Nat is at the same time aware of their rage and their burdens, they remind him of the utter hopelessness of their condition. Their cheerfulness is crushed and blighted by their bondage to the white society. This ignites his fury, and his thoughts leap to Daniel's beast that will appear on the last violent days.

A slave in ante-bellum America had no legal existence beyond that of a chattel. The names of the slaves are mentioned in plantation account books, in notices of slave auctions or in newspaper advertisements offering slaves for hire or rewards for runaways. There is hardly any glimpse of humanity beneath these statistical records. Gray, the white lawyer reminds Nat of his precarious existence as a chattel in a white dominated society.

The point is that you are animate chattel and animate chattel is capable of craft and connivery and wily stealth.

> You ain't a wagon, Reverend, but chattel that possess moral choice and spiritual volition. Remember that well. Because that's how some law provides that animate chattel like you can be tried for, a felony, and that's how come you're goin' to be tried next Sattidy. (21-22)

Though the slave as animate chattel is credited with moral choice and spiritual volition, the white society has made a slave too weak-minded to realize the significance of such spiritual language. Ironically, the system would not countenance the possession of moral choice and spiritual volition to illumine the unique existence of slave as a human being but only to get the right to punish him. Nat realises that every Negro is "only merchandise, goods, in the eyes of all white people devoid of character of moral sense of soul." (53) This awareness comes into focus with all the force of immediacy as Nat meditates on the intrinsic worth of Hark, his associate in the rebellion. Now lodged in the cell next to his, Hark is about to die on the gallows. Nat reflects:

> . . . had he been able to read and write, been *White*, *free*, living in some Elysian time when he was anything but negotiable property worth six hundred dollars in a depressed market, he might have been a lawyer. (53) (emphasis added)

Nat is very much conscious that he and his people like Hark cannot *belong* since "being white" and "being free" always go together in the white society. Living in a world to which he cannot belong, a slave is condemned to play a role constantly. Happiness is assured to a slave in his total anonymity bordering on non-existence. Nat realises this when he thinks of the course his life would have taken, had he lived like an ordinary slave:

> . . . I would doubtless have become an ordinary run-of-the-mill house nigger, mildly efficient at some stupid task like wringing chicken's necks or smoking hams or polishing silver . . . growing ever more servile and unctuous as I

> become older, always the crafty flatterer on the lookout for some bonus of flannel or stew beef or tobacco, yet behind my stately paunch and fancy bib and waistcoat developing, as I advanced into old age, a kind of purse-lipped dignity, known as Uncle Nat, well loved and adoring in return, a palsied stroker of the silken pates of little white grandchildren, rheumatic, illiterate, and filled with sleepiness, half yearning for that lonely death which at long last would lead me to rest in some tumble down graveyard tangled with chokeberry and jimson weed. It would not have been, to be sure, much of an existence, but how can I honestly say that I might not have been happier ? (155-56)

Nat knows the cost of this comfort in terms of human worth. The constant role playing exacts heavy toll in psychological expense. The total dehumanizing effect of monstrous slavery has reduced man's life to a cipher.

Nat is aware of the unspeakable misery of slaves in the South. He is depressed by the feeling that there is no way out. His keen sensitivity is exacerbated as he looks at Tom and Andrew struggling with a painfully heavy burden of the crude oken timbers:

> *Ah* ! they fell as I watched, tumbling down with a lumpish clatter. Then slowly the blessed nincompoops rearranged the sawhorses into a stack again, hoisted them up and continued their hunched and lead-footed pilgrimage across the field, two raggedy silhouettes against a frieze of pinewoods and wintry sky, bound as if for nowhere on to the limits of the earth—black faceless paradigms of an absurd and immemorial futility. It gave a quick shiver in the chill and thought: Why do men live at all ? Why do men wrassle so with air, with nothing ? (327)

The terrible anguish brings him the realisation that the slave's life including his own is denied human worth. This awareness is further aggravated when he confronts the tragic waste of human element and all its promise stifled by slavery. In his dark cell he reflects;

> . . . a fly must be one of the most fortunate of God's creatures. Brainless born, brainlessly seeking its sustenance from anything wet and warm, it found its brainless mate, reproduced, and died brainless, unacquainted with misery or grief. But then I asked myself: how could I be sure ? Who could say that flies were not instead God's supreme outcastes, buzzing eternally between heaven and oblivion in a pure agony of mindless twitching forced by instinct to dine off sweat and slime and offal, their very brainlessness an everlasting torment ? So that even if someone, well-meaning but mistaken wished himself out of human misery and into a fly's estate, he would only find himself in a more monstrous hell than he had even imagined—an existence in which there was no act of will, no choice, but a blind and automatic obedience to instinct which caused him to feast endlessly and gluttonously and revoltingly upon the guts of a rotting fox or a bucket of prisoner's slops. Surely then, that would be the ultimate damnation: to exist in the world of a fly, eating thus, without will or choice and against all desire. (26-27)

Slavery condemns man to the ultimate damnation stifling his will and negating his desire. Nat constantly evaluates the loss of human worth and dignity under the system. This awareness has made him the sensitive outsider who reflects on the effect of slavery with sympathy and compassion. Enclosed in slavery, one is condemned helplessly to conscious role-playing or a stupid will-less existence like a fly fatting on slime and offal. This smug existence is again worse than death since life is deprived of its essence.

Nat further reveals the tragic fact that a slave has no will even to end his life: the only way open to him to get out of the enclosing walls of intolerable existence. The deprivation of will to commit suicide has brought a slave on a par with vegetable or animal existence. It was not his Christian faith that sustained him in the midst of inhuman adversity. It was not "a kind of righteousness at the heart of suffering, and the will toward patience and forbearance in the knowledge of life." (27) It is in fact the proof of total negation of humanity that Negroes lacked "even that will to destroy by their own hand their unending anguish." (27) A slave is condemned to live without significance.

The other great assault on slave's human worth was the callous break-up of families. This becomes a major causative factor of violence. Even the genial tempered Hark is inflamed when he remembers how his wife Tiny and little son Lucas were sold to south by his master Joseph Travis without qualms of conscience although it was not "a killing sacrifice for him to feed two more mouths." (341) Hark blurts out: "I knows I kin kill." (353) Nat can never forget the ravishing of his mother by a drunken Irish overseer. It has always haunted his mind, and he remembers the way he felt "a sense of my weakness, my smallness, my defenselessness, my *niggerness* invading me like a wind to the marrow of my bones." (150) He remembers the cruelty meted out to Will, Nelson, Sam and Henry. Will made into woods unable to bear the tortures of his master and was subsequently tracked and inhumanly beaten into submission. He has "the frenzied, mindless quality of a wild boar hog cornered hopelessly in a thicket." (102) Henry was rendered completely deaf by a blow on the head from a drunken overseer and its recollection "feeds his calm fury." (103)

Because of his education and sensitivity Nat realizes that he cannot win freedom for himself alone. His experience has taught him that he cannot step out while the slavery existed. Styron recreates the institution of slavery by references to the wretchedness of freed slaves like Arnold and Isham. They have got out of slavery only to become more wretched. The case of Arnold becomes a powerful indictment of what slavery has done to Negroes as a whole. Arnold with "his spirit numbed by the forty years or more he had spent as a chattel" (261) lived in his freedom "upon life's farthest rim, more insignificant and wretched than he had ever been in slavery."(261) He has now come to experience a worse kind of slavery in his meaningless freedom as he has become a simple beggar and the townsmen "no longer his masters in fact but in spirit masters more tyrannical than ever before" (261). Nat comes to regard him as:

> —a symbol of something gone asunder in the institution yet even more importantly a walking reminder of freedom

> itself and of menacing words, rarely spoken aloud, like emancipation and manumission. . . he was still the incarnation of freedom, and such freedom was, as any fool could see, a striking apparition of hopelessness and degradation. (261)

Styron creates a powerful episode as Arnold confronts a beautiful Northern lady arriving as a fiance of Marsee Ridley. The lady asks directions of Arnold who is incapable of speaking or understanding. He merely mumbles most pitifully in an incoherent way. She is confused and upset by the horror of guilt and remorse.

> For the woman said nothing more, simply stood there while her arm went limp and the parasol clattered to the road, then raised her clenched fists to her face as if she were striking herself—an angry tormented gesture—and burst into tears. Her whole frame—backbone, shoulders, rib cage—all the bones which moments before had supported her so proudly seemed to collapse inward with a rush, and she became helpless and shrunken as she stood there in the road, fists pressed to her eyes, shaken by loud racking sobs. It was as if something long pent up within her had been loosed in a torrent. (263)

The whole scene has a great impact on Nat. He is "seized by a hot convulsive emotion." (263) He realises that "the occasional expressions of sympathy" are incongruous and grotesque in the midst of unspeakable human tragedy. He resolves to break the barriers of false sentimentality and abject fear by forcing his violent self on whites. He interprets the white woman's pity as a provocation to break the barrier.

> For what I had seen on this white woman's face was pity—pity wrenched from the very depths of her soul—and the sight of that pity, the vision of that tender self so reduced by compassion to this helpless state of sobs and bloodless clenched knuckles and scalding tears, caused me an irresistible, flooding moment of desire. And it was, you see, pity

> alone that did this, not the woman herself apart from pity. (263-64)

Nat's rage is the force that should rise above all personal and human considerations. Violence would manifest itself when it can thrust itself unhampered by the other counteracting human factors like pity or compassion. Nat rejects "pity" whenever it shows itself in various forms. He is, therefore, ready to celebrate and appreciate the profound quality of rage that Isham exemplifies as he confronts and curses Nat's degenerate master Moore.

Isham, a destitute free Negro, diseased and impoverished with a family of eight to support went to work with Nat's illiterate master Moore. The white man turned him out without paying his wages. Moore and his cousin on their way to Jerusalem come across Isham holding a child close to death. Isham confronts them with burning rage and raw hatred and his cursing words "assailed them like bullwhip." (297) Nat watched the frightened discomfiture of the White man. He reflects on this experience:

> I realised that Isham's unbelievable words had at first thrust Moore into a strange new world of consciousness which lacked a name—so strange an emotion indeed that a long moment must have passed while voice called to voice across the squalid abysm inside his skull and finally named it: Terror. (298)

The "terror" reveals the hollowness of White brave front. Nat has a glimpse of the power of rage which would make white men "Toad stool-White" with fear. He is forced to realise that "people whose skins were black would never find liberty—never, never so long as men like Moore dwelt on God's earth." (298). The pure hatred has become in his mind an unfailing instrument to strike terror into white man's flinty bosom. The fearless fury of "a famished Negro so drained of life's juices that he lacked even the spittle to spit," (298) has shown the way. He silentiy admires "the hopeless and proud and unrelenting fury of Isham." (298)

The juxtaposition of the white woman's pity and Isham's fury serve to define Nat's philosophy of violence. He comes to the couclusion that white man's pity and charity ignite his "murderous hatred" more than his abuse or scorn. Pity and charity have no place in his fight with the monstrous institution of slavery. The pure hatred alone would become an unfailing source of violence. A negro cannot nurse pure hatred without an intimate knowledge of White man's life, his arrogant kindness, his hypocrisy, his lust and his dirt. Without knowing these he can only pretend hatred and "Such hatred is an abstraction of a delusion." (258) Nat learns the secret of silent and informed fury and believes that a Negro can hate perfectly only when he inculcates in himself "that calm and intelligent and unrepenting purity of hatred." Negro's intimacy with white man will give him

> Real hatred of the sort of which I speak—hatred so pure and obdurate that no sympathy, no human warmth, no flicker of compassion can make the faintest nick or scratch upon the stony surface of its being. . . . Like a flower of granite with cruel leaves it grows, when it grows at all, as if from fragile seed cast upon uncertain ground. (254)

Nat speaks of "the full fruition of this hatred" and "its ripe and malevolent growth" as requisites to wreck the institution of slavery.

Nat's identification with the blacks takes shape slowly. His homosexual union with Willis is looked upon as the spiritual binding of two souls and Nat construes it as "*The soul of Jonathan was knit with the soul of David, and Jonathan loved him as his own soul.*" Nat and Willis become inseparable in spiritual kinship. Nat's disappointment is acute as Samuel Turner sells away Willis to South making Nat an innocent accomplice in the sad affair. Nat feels the sordidness of slavery as he comes across the slave coffle of about forty Negro men and boys linked to each other by chains. Their helplessness deeply hurts him. Raymond of the scoffle reminds Nat that he was after all a Negro no matter how favoured he was temporarily. He could not be free from the disadvantages of his race.

He was permanently bound with them. His fate was linked with theirs. He was on a par with them. Raymond shouts prophetically: "Yo' shit stink too, sugah. Yo' ass black jes' like mine, honey chile" (201). The words have terrible effect on Nat. They bring home the fact that he cannot hope freedom for himself alone as the system existed and operated in all its cruelty.

Nat is far superior to his white masters who are illiterate, degenerate and wily. His predicament is thus all the more unbearable. He views from this vantage point the loss of human potentialities wasted by the white tyranny. The blasphemous incestuous couplings of Miss Emmeline with her cousin in the hayfield shock him into awareness that the black and white are hardly distinguished in moral depravity. The duplicity of the white race is further obvious in their religious hypocrisy portrayed in the novel through the mindless arrogance and bigotry of Richard Whitehead. The religious minister even volunteers to track down and shoot Will who ran away from his barbarously cruel master Nathaniel Francis. Richard shows his mean contempt for Nat when the latter seeks permission to baptize Ethelred Brantley. This religious personage is ready to curse. He cannot bless. The failure of religion in its travesty not only infuriates Nat, it also shows him the need to rip the unholy mask. Nat's purity and spiritual commitment urge him to baptize the degenerate and helpless white man Ethelred Brantley. Richard Whitehead's refusal stands out in contrast. Styron carefully proves that the white community was on the whole effete and far inferior to Nat and inevitably brought ruin on itself by insisting on his continued slavery. The narration moves on to the climax as events march to the inevitable emergence of violence as the only way out. Nat as a votary of violence has to make the categorisation complete—to identify himself with the Blacks and bring destruction to the whites. He would swiftly do away with the factors that might come in the way of these neat and clearly defined categorisations. The easier his circumstances become, the more furious he becomes. He confronts pity with vengeance to sustain his philosophy. Nat is convinced that the atrocities and cruelties inflicted on Negro are taken in their stride with quiet acceptance as they are integrated with the system. Once the slave becomes aware of his existence as possible beyond the confines of the system he is bound to become a violent rebel. Styron makes it clear that Samuel Turner with his well-meaning philanthropy is no less responsible for Nat's violence than those who inflicted inhuman tortures of slavery on his person and soul. Nat finds it impossible to explain to Thomas Gray, his white confessor when the latter asks him as to why he killed "A man who you admit is kind and gentle to you and you butcher in cold blood." (34) Nat is unable to reply "not because there was no reply to the question," but chiefly because Gray, grafted to the system can neither understand nor appreciate Nat's philosophy of violence born of "pure" hatred.

Therefore Nat's readiness to murder Joseph Tarvis is in effect a ritual murder of Samuel Turner, his benefactor. Samuel Turner tickled him with hope of freedom and finally, though helplessly, he tricked him into infernal thraldom. Nat knows that the sporadic acts of kindness through Turner and Margaret were futile and ineffectual and cannot break the inhuman barriers. On the contrary, they tend to make a slave's life more miserable. Therefore, Nat hates Turner and kills Margaret. Nat wants to end the very system. Nat's consciousness of freedom as a human right enables him to identify himself with the Blacks and to liberate them through violence which is the only means to accomplish it.

Nat's experience of Negroes' life at the market opens floodgates of fury. Nathaniel Francis in a drunken state eggs on his slaves Will and Sam to fight each other for the amusement of white trash. Both of them end up pitifully bleeding and exhausted. Nat finds it unendurable:

> My heart, as I say, shrank inside me, died, disappeared, and rage like a newborn child exploded there to fill the void: it was at this instant that I knew beyond doubt or danger that—whatever the place, whatever the appointed time, whoever the gentle young girl now serenely plucking blossoms within a bower or the mistress knitting in the coolness of a country parlor or the innocent lad seated contemplating the cobwebbed walls of an outhouse in a summery

> field—the whole world of white flesh would someday founder and split apart upon my retribution, would perish by my design and at my hands. My stomach heaved and I restrained the urge to vomit on the boards where I sat. (306-307)

Styron very convincingly reveals the stark inhumanity of slavery which drives Nat to see himself "black as the blackest vengeance, the illimitable, devastating instrument of God's wrath," (52) and welcomes Ezekiel's divine fury:

> . . . *Slay utterly old and young both maids and little children, and woman* . . .

The most depressing factor about salvery is that the slaves fail to appreciate the value of freedom. Nat begins to view slaves in the context of white life around. In the initial stages of his understanding, he is appalled by their hopelessly ugly and revolting way of life. He hates their slovenliness, their filth and their pitiful superstitions. Their total submission to the white masters and their readiness to betray their own kith and kin, and their petty jealousies infuriate him. Yet he understands that they could not help being what they are in the grinding mill of slavery. Styron describes in detail the runaway slaves being betrayed by the Blacks, and the Blacks spying on one another. He makes Nat realize finally that his bloody mission failed miserably not merely because the slaves did not join but because of the crushing fact that the slaves had fought against their own in defense of their soul-less white masters. Nat would even curse in sheer despair that the slaves deserve their miseries richly because of their wretched lack of feeling for one another. Styron's portrayal of Nat parallels Milton's Samson who "eyeless at Gaza working at the mill with slaves," realises that the Israelites for whom he fought under God's direction hand merely disowned him. Yet there is a basic difference between the two in spite of the rich Biblical parallelisms. Samson's hate is un-qualified, reproachful and egocentric, Nat's dismissal of fellow slaves is tinged with compassion. He would not blame them. He would merely understand their predicament as social inevitability, and pity the slaves ground down ruthlessly by the juggernaut of slavery. He is in the end convinced that the little he did was much in the light of the insuperable barriers around. He was glad that he made a dent into the system. He has no regrets for his failure and for the whole-sale murder of helpless women, little children and even the infant sleeping in the cradle. He would not feel guilty. He would do it all over again were he given a chance. He is clear in his conscience. He would not plead guilty since there is no guilt in ending the cruel system of slavery and those who perpetrate inhuman indignities on helpless beings. Judged from the sociological point of view, violence has redeemed him. He has merely done his duty as a sincere and sensitive human being who acts out of irrepressible compassion for his fellow beings.

The institution of slavery is violent by its total negative dehumanizing stance, and therefore begets violence. The sociological aspect of violence ably brought out through various points of view revealing the whole landscape, the life lived in the particular period of history and finally the forces converging to make violence inevitable. On the first level of interpretation, Nat as a slave views slavery and decides to strike. The historicity of Nat and the institution of slavery are necessary to the extent they provide the framework and pattern for the various forces that were heading fast to a violent culmination: the stupidity of white masters, the economic compulsions, the blighting of Virginia, and the consequent uneasy tensions between the races. Styron recreates the 19th century Virginia and the horrors of the institution of slavery with unremitting fidelity to explain the emergence of a sensitive human being as the bloodiest rebel.

The authenticity of the historic background has made the Southern historian Vann Woodward describe the novel as "the most profound treatment we have had of slavery in our literature. And the only one that tells the story from the slave's point of view."[32]

III

Nat is more than a slave and his revolt is more than a sociological fact. When all the sociological strands are verified and separated from the fabric, yet the central mystique of the novel remains. Nat's stature grows beyond slavery and he merits the definition of a tragic hero. Though the historicity is integral to this purpose, Styron's protagonist is extremely complex. Nat is a Christ figure, a religious agonist and a criminal saint dramatizing through his intense personal struggle modern human tragedy.

Styron has gone beyond the sociological concerns. If he simply stopped at the successful portrayal of the slavery in the 19th century Virginia, the novel would have shaped itself as an angry protest of considerable literary merit. Styron's objective is not to write a story of historically real episode of violence. It would have been a historical novel and not a meditation on history. The artistic meditation on history should reveal the quality of human life in an exceptionally sensitive protagonist who would by his extraordinary awareness of tragedy redeems history and his own self. This has necessitated a journey into the self which is the battleground of violence and vengeance on the one hand and charity and compassion, on the other. The Old Testament vengeance and the New Testament brotherhood come to converge as well-defined polarities and leave Nat a chastened tragic hero. Styron has, therefore, made his novel a religious tragedy and also a psychosexual drama as he has to speak of human reaction to sociological reality in a given period of history.

In this context Nat's religious fervour and the episode of Margaret Whitehead fit the pattern. Styron has deliberately shaped the religious element of Nat as evidenced in original *Confessions* to turn Nat's story into a fable of Fall and Redemption. Nat becomes "man alone" with his extraordinary psychological sensitivity and awareness. Styron reveals this through Nat's religious fundamentalism. Nat is far more well-versed in the Bible and deeply involved in religion than all his masters. Styron explores Nat's relationship with God very sensitively revealing subtly the travesty of religion by the established church in various ways. Denied freedom in the society, Nat seeks fulfilment through God and "visions" and "Dreams" through which he realises identity as a human being, internalizing the grim reality with an acceptable religious form. Nat has seen the failure of all his paternal figures, especially through the denial of freedom. His need is to get out of the world with which he cannot communicate. This is accomplished in the first place by reversing the values of the insensitive society: the black becomes good and white evil. Compassion is replaced by vengeance. Nat's prior adoration for white men has changed into love for the blacks. His yearning to equal the whites gets transformed into an imperative need to assert his identity in the violent destruction of the whites. The Blacks become in his view far superior to the whites. He inspires his people to be proud of their blackness. He hates "the white man's wiles, his duplicity, his greediness; and his ultimate depravity." Whiteness is a hypocritical covering of the inner prurience. This not only marks the end of his spiritual subjugation to the whites; it also betokens the collapse of all the comforting symbols. He earns the agonising isolation which leads him to "the ultimate paternal symbol, that is God, to embrace him."[33] From this moment on, he views his experience entirely in religious terms, in visions and dreams.

Styron introduces the vision of promontory in the beginning of the novel. It provides a profound commentary on Nat's complex spiritual yearning for freedom. Even though he fails to spell out his psychic imperatives, he poignantly visualizes them in his vision. He narrates:

> Now as I drift near the cape I raise my eyes to the promontory facing out upon the sea. There again I see what I know I will see, as always. In the sunlight the building stands white—stark white and serene against a blue and cloudless sky. It is square and formed of marble, like a temple, and is simply designed, possessing no columns or windows but rather, in place of them, recesses whose purpose I cannot imagine, flowing in a series of arches around its two visible sides. The building has no door, at least there is no door

> that I can see. Likewise, just as this building possesses neither doors nor windows, it seems to have no purpose, resembling as I say, a temple—yet a temple in which no one worships, or a sarcophagus in which no one lies buried, or a monument to something mysterious, ineffable, and without name. But as is my custom whenever I have this dream or vision, I don't dwell upon the meaning of the strange building standing so lonely and remote upon its ocean promontory, for it seems by its very purposelessness to be endowed with a profound mystery which to explore would yield only a profusion of darker and perhaps more troubling mysteries, as in a maze. (4)

The promontory symbolizes his heightened aspirations for something beyond his reach. The pursuit of it has involved him in "profound mystery" of existence, his own and others's. The paradigmatic passage sets the tone of narration and acts as an expanding symbol throughout the novel. The vision explicates itself as events unfold the story. Nat is a hopeless pilgrim of unattainable freedom. He would not dwell upon the meaning of the strange building because he cannot understand it till it is realized in the violent climax of events. The vision becomes relevant and meaningful only in retrospect. His longing for freedom and his conviction that violence is the only means to get it, are thus inextricably bound with each other right from the start. Yet the realisation of freedom alone would end the agony of "the animate chatte." The unspeakable misery of slaves is revealed to him in a dream which is in sharp contrast with his vision of promontory:

> Suddenly another sound came to my ears, this time the frightened outcry of the voices. They were the voices of boys, hoarse and half grown and seized with terror, and now instantly I saw them: half a dozen black boys trapped neck-deep in a bog of quick-sand, crying aloud for rescue as their arms waved frantically in the dim light and as they sank deeper and deeper into the mire. I seemed to stand helpless at the edge of the bog, unable to move or to speak, and while I stood there a voice echoed out of the

> sky, itself partaking of that remote sound of thunder: *Thy sons shall be given unto another people and thine eyes shall look, and fail with longing for them all the day long, so that thou shalt be mad for the sight of thine eyes* . . . Screaming their mortal fright, black arms and faces sinking beneath the slime, the boys began to vanish one by one before my eyes while the noise of a prodigious guilt overwhelmed me like a thunderlap. . . . (76)

Nat holds himself implicated in the helplessness of the slaves. They are hopelessly lost as they are denied freedom. He has ranged himself to deliver them from bondage. The promontory continues to be mysterious and the nightmarish "sinking in the bog" of the slaves is a painful fact. He feels "a prodigious guilt" as he sustains the conflict between the intention of freedom (vision) and the reality of unending bondage (nightmare). The vision of promontory is the only key to the nightmare of the Negro boys sinking in the quagmire. The melodramatic constructs gain importance in the context of Nat's religious fervour. Nat's relationship with God is thus vital in the assessment of his entire being. Styron has made the point explicit:

> The major reason was, however, that I wanted to get Nat after the insurrection when he was questioning the entire relationship he had with God, with the God who had been his guide and mentor and light throughout his life as a preacher. I wanted to discover what was going on in his mind, now that he had instigated and committed murder, and now that he is bereft of God. The relationship with God seemed to be the central thing in my own conception of the man.[34]

Styron has put Nat in jail with the absence of God racking his heart. Nat feels that God has deserted him after his only murder. He has killed Margaret Whitehead who had shown him sympathy and pity in her life. She was in fact the only white who had treated him as a human being. Even Samuel Turner who encouraged Nat to learn a trade and earn his freedom, treated him as "an experiment." The real human sympathy and pity Nat experiences only in his confrontation with Margaret Whitehead—the sixteen year old daughter of Catherine Whitehead who often had Nat on hire from Joseph Trovis in exchange for a pair of oxen. Styron brings Nat and Margaret close to reveal the inhumanity of the plantation society which successfully stamped out sympathy and compassion. Margaret symbolizes purity in all its aspects—love, charity and compassion. In his fury Nat failed to realize the overmastering power of compassion which he confronts all of a sudden while dealing violently not with abstract concepts but with human beings. Nat's humanity asserts. Negation of freedom through Samuel Turner and negation of love through Margaret make him acutely conscious of the need to affirm his identity in a society that denies it. Violence becomes the means of affirmation. Styron writes:

> The barrier is incredible, but it's tissue paper thin, and for just that reason it is all the more impermeable. And so the way that you break it down is in the most apocalyptic way that is possible to a human being. You break through it by killing. And it seems to me that it is symbolic of the human condition.[35]

Nat emerges from the bog by striking a violent blow. He would win his identity by the spilling of white blood. The situation very close to Gothic crudity is saved by the astonishing manipulation of grisly massacre. Nat Turner and his men have come to kill Joseph Travis and his wife in sleep. Later Nat reflects in jail:

> Now I saw that beneath the perplexity, the film of sleep, his eyes were brown and rather melancholy, acquainted with hard toil, remote perhaps, somewhat inflexible but not at all unkind, and I felt that I knew him at last. . . . It was as if by encountering those eyes I had found the torn and long missing fragment of a portrait of this far-off abstract being who possessed my body; his face was complete now and I had a final glimpse of who he truly might be. *Whatever else he was, he was a man.* (387-88) (emphasis added)

The concrete reality of dealing with a human being has revealed the emptiness of all the abstract formulations. Though Nat stifles his humanity momentarily, he confronts the fact that he cannot be the vengeful black angel he wants to be. The intimate human reality swoops into his consciousness with a telling effect, and forces Nat to come out of his visionary obsessions and categorisations. He fails to kill. His lieutenant Will "the executioner" dispatches the white man.

Styron has faced a difficult problem in creating unconscious sexual tension between the young Nat and unintentionally flirtatious Margaret. The entire episode is designed to uncover "the cost of maintaining purity which is an abstraction from the rest of life."[36] Styron builds the episode on the intriguing fact that Margaret was the only girl Nat killed. Styron believes that there must have been "a very guarded sexual relationship"[37] between Nat and Margaret because both were young, religious and there was also the fact of "the rather easy going sort of racial relationships of the time."[38] Nat and Margaret meet often as Nat is hired out to her family. He drives her coach while she is visiting her friends. Driving through a deserted part of the country while she is pouring out her appreciation, Nat feels:

> Again I smelled the warm girl-sweat, sensed her presence, soap, skin, hair lavender. Suddenly, despite myself, the godless thought came: I could stop now and here, right here by the road in this meadow, do with her anything I wished. There's not a soul for miles. I could throw her down and spread her young white legs and stick myself in her until belly met belly and shoot inside her in warm milky spurts of desecration. And let her scream until the empty pinewoods echoed to her cries and no one would be the wiser, not even the buzzards or the crows. . . . The sweat poured down my sides beneath my shirt. Then I uttered a silent prayer, and furiously thrust the thought out of my mind as one thrusts away the very body and spirit of Satan. (367)

Nat experiences violent lust and also passionate urge to curb it at once lest it should hinder "my great mission." The mission to kill the whites is a divine duty, and all that comes in the way of its execution should be regarded as "Satanic" including pity and compassion since they blunt the edge of violence. The more violent Nat comes the nearer he feels towards God, as he is convinced that vengeance is divinely ordained. He nurses his fury. The proximity of Margaret and her solitude bring to his mind "a minor but thorny problem" facing him—whether he should kill or spare his master Travis and more particularly his wife Sarah when he launches his massacre :

> I had resolved on a mercilessly intransigent course of action when it came to killing the white people, determined that not a single soul—no matter how friendly our relations had been—would be spared the axe or the gun. To contemplate otherwise might be fatal, for if I allowed my heart to soften in the case of one person, it would be all too easy for such clemency to overtake me with another and still another. (369)

Nat is fashioning himself into an instrument of God's wrath and vengeance. He has to negate charity and compassion in order to fulfil his mission because his fight was not against human beings but against an obnoxious system that degraded them.

During the journey Margaret finds a turtle crushed by a passing wagon or cart and insists that the poor thing should be put out of suffering. Nat says :

> I found a hickory branch at the side of the road and smote the head of the turtle hard, a single time; its legs and tail quivered briefly, then relaxed with a soft uncurling motion, the tail drooped, and it was dead. When I threw the stick into the field and turned back to Margaret, I saw that her lips were trembling. (370)

Margaret becomes dizzy and walks to a nearby brook with Nat. While talking she suddenly trips and falls against Nat for the briefest instant. He feels "inconsolable with emptiness such as I have never known." (374)

Her proximity and her sympathy tease him once again beyond endurance when Margaret wearing pantalettes not yet concealed by a skirt bursts into the library where Nat is working on bookshelves. Nat has cut his finger. Her indifference to Nat's presence as a male rouses his anger, "had I not been a Negro and therefore presumably unstirred by such a revealing sight, she would never be so immodest to flaunt thus beneath my nose." (337) When suddenly she finds that Nat is bleeding, she holds his "unwounded right hand." Nat jerks his hand away and protests that the wound is just simple. Before she leaves, she promises him the five pennies she would get from her friend as she has won the bet in a dispute about a passage in the Bible, with Nat's help. The paternalistic solicitation and condescension ignite in Nat desire and rage. His rage springs from his awareness of her inaccessibility. He finds in her "a denial of his full dignity as a man."[39] She becomes, as Donald Markos remarks, "the symbol of his frustration and reminder of his emasculation."[40] Nat's rebellion is a reaction to this emasculation. Margaret makes Nat fully conscious of the slave's position in the white system. Nat had to revolt to assert his manhood and his full dignity as a man. Margaret is the source of his greatest torment. Nat strikes her down. This is the inevitable tragic outcome of the social condition.

The whole episode of Margaret is carefully designed. The killing of turtle closely parallels Nat's murder of Margaret with a fence rail:

> Then when I raised the rail above her head she gazed at me, as if past the imponderable vista of her anguish, with a grave and drowsy tenderness such as I had never known, spoke some words too soft to hear and, saying no more, closed her eyes upon all madness, illusion, error, dream and strife. So I brought the timber down and she was swiftly gone, and I hurled the hateful, shattered club far up into the weeds. (414-15)

The hickory stick that despatched the turtle was simply thrown into woods as "Turtle don't feel anything." (370) Nat vividly remembers and narrates the episode specially repeating Margaret's remark, "It's just—oh, suffering things." (370) Nat has no pity for the turtle. He tries hard not to feel compassion for Margaret, the suffering human being who showed him the path of compassion through her spontaneous gesture. He fails as his humanity asserts. The instrument of his only murder becomes "the hateful shattered club." The whole act of vengeance becomes empty and meaningless revealing the life as "all madness, illusion, error, dream, and strife." (415) He says:

> By the edge of the woods I found myself seated on a log, head in my hands, unaccountably thinking of ancient monuments of childhood—warm rain, leaves, a whippoorwill, rushing mill wheels, Jews harp strumming—centuries before. Then I arose again and resumed my meaningless and ordained circuit of her body, not near it yet ever within sight as if that crumpled blue were the center of an orbit around whose path I must make a ceaseless pilgrimage. (415)

In the murder of Margaret, he confronts the terrible shattering of "ancient monuments of childhood." Violence has emptied the meaning of it all. Margaret reminds him of the expense and value of life he has missed in his mad vengeful fury. She becomes "the centre of an orbit" and an object of ceaseless pilgrimage like the white promontory of his vision. The death of Margaret is the disintegration of the vision and also of his mission. He moves on listlessly. He cannot kill. He sees a young white girl of fourteen or so escape into the woods. Her escape ruins Nat's revolt. Nat tells:

> I might have reached her in a twinkling—the work of half a minute—but I suddenly felt dispirited and overcome by fatigue, and was pursued by an obscure, unshakable grief. I shivered in the knowledge of the futility of all ambition. My mouth was sour with the yellow recollection of death and blood-smeared fields and walls. I watched the girl slip away, vanish without a hand laid upon her. Who knows but whether we were not doomed to lose. I know nothing

> any longer. Nothing. Did I really wish to vouchsafe a life for the one that I had taken ? (417)

Nat's vengeance is powerless against his compassionate understanding of life. He was not made for violence and vengeance. His pity for Brantley, his sorrow for Jeremiah Cobb and his recognition of enemy as "a man" would never make him an instrument of remorseless vengeance. His soul is inevitably made for the conflict between impersonal violence and personal compassion. Deeply religious as his life was, his evolution is "as a ceaseless pilgrimage" from one aspect of God to another. The conflict takes the dimensions of a drama between man and God. Styron has said:

> the book . . . is a sort of religious parable and a story of exculpation. . . It should be apparent that the book expresses the idea of Old Testament savagery and revenge redeemed by New Testament charity and brotherhood.[41]

Nat moves from the vengeful aspect of God. He can come back to Him when he touches the other aspect: compassion. As he was convinced of "God's wrath," he was ready to kill. The act of murder revealed its inadequacy as an attribute of God and also of man. Nat, therefore, hates Will's brutality and finds it revolting because it is devoid of human values. It is, in fact, symbolic of a moral destructive forces that do not respond to and cannot be tempered by compassion. Nat's violence on the contrary is to serve human values. It fails when it negates compassion. After his only murder Nat feels deserted:

> . . . when I went back to the border of the woods and knelt there to ask God's guidance in the coming time of solitude—to request that he show me the ways and necessities for my salvation now that my cause in His name was irrevocably lost—I found to my terrible distress that for the first time in my life I was unable even to think. Try as I might, I could not cause a prayer to pass my lips. *The*

> *God I knew* was slipping away from me. (402) (emphasis added)

The desertion of God causes him great anguish as "*The God I knew*" was no longer the answer. He is unable to pray. He feels nevertheless that "by this silence and absence, He is giving me a greater sign than any *I have ever known.*" (402) (emphasis added) His knowledge of the other aspect of God alone would bring him to God.

The last part of the novel "It is Done," is very carefully planned to make Nat's pilgrimage complete. He now knows God's love, charity and compassion which he would not have known but for his one murder. Nat's attitude to Gray who has come to give him the Bible against the will of the court, hints at the change:

> He hands the Bible to me through the bars of the door. For a long moment we gaze at each other in the flickering light and I have a strange sensation which passes almost as quickly as it comes, that never have I seen this man in my life. I say nothing to him in answer. At last he reaches through the bars and grasps my hand; as he does so I know by some strange and tentative feeling in his hasty grip that this is the first black hand he has ever shaken, no doubt the last. (425)

Both Nat and Gray are touched by the spirit that is beyond the confines of racial prejudice and violence. They are compassionate to each other. As Gray is gone:

> I turn and place the Bible down gently on the cedar plank. I know that I would not open it now even if I had the light to read it by. Yet its presence warms the cell and for the first time since I have been in jail, for the first time since I gazed into his irksome face, *I feel a wrench of pity for Gray* and for his mortal years to come. (425) (emphasis added)

The power of compassion lifts Gray and Cobb above the ordinary confines of law. Sentencing Nat to death on the gallows—Judge Cobb observes: "from my soul I pity you, and while you have my sympathies I am nevertheless called upon to pass sentence of the court." (106) Nat reflects:

> We gazed at each other from vast distances, yet close, awesomely close, as if shining for the briefest instant some rare secret—unknown to other men—of all time, all mortality and sin and grief. (106)

As the day of his execution dawns, gazing up at the morning star, Nat experiences an autistic Union with Margaret :

> And as I think of her, the desire swells within me and I am stirred by a longing so great that like those memories of time past and long-ago voices, flowing waters, rushing winds, it seems more than my heart can abide. *Beloved, let us love one another: for love is of God, and everyone that loveth is born of God, and knoweth God.* Her voice is close, familiar, real, and for an instant I mistake the wind against my ear, a gentle gust, for her breath, and I turn to seek her in the darkness. And now beyond my fear, beyond my dread and emptiness, I feel the warmth flow into my loins and my legs tingle with desire. I tremble and I search for her face in my mind, seek her young body, yearning for her suddenly with a rage that racks me with a craving beyond pain; with tender stroking motions I pour out my love within her; pulsing flood; she arches against me, cries out, and the twain—black and white—are one. I faint slowly. My head falls toward the window, my breath comes hard. I recall a meadow, June, the voice of a whisper: *Is it true, Nat ? Did he not say, I am the root and offspring of David, and the bright aud morning star* ? (426)

She returns to him in his imagination with the message of love, because love is the knowledge of God. He is now convinced of the meaning and value of life, and emerges from darkness to view "the bright and morning star." In the last few pages Styron has fused several symbols, the morning star, the marble temple and Margaret into one. Nat knows the mystery of the marble temple as black and white are one. He knows love and compassion and therefore God. He is not "racked with the deep despair" of Satan hurled far from God. He finds the meaning of his life and mission through Margaret, the symbol of compassion. He has found his redemption in her crucifixion. Thus the act of murder becomes the act of affirmation.

Nat goes to his death uncontrite and with hope. He has no sense of guilt.

> *I would have done it all again. I would have destroyed them all. Yet I would have spared one. I would have spared her that showed me Him whose presence I had not fathomed or maybe never even known. Great God, how early it is! Until now I had almost forgotten His name*: (428)

His ability to pray returns. The call of the executioner comes to him in the Christly notes of compassion.

> "Come!" the voice booms, but commanding me now:
> *Come, My son*! I turn in surrender.
> Surely I come quickly. Amen.
> Even so, come, Lord Jesus.
> Oh how bright and fair the moring star . . . (428)

While Nat's compassion for slaves renders his violence an affirmative act sociologically, Margaret's crucifixion transform it into a redemptive act symbolically. Styron has made the violent rebellion into a parable of compassion and exculpation. In delineating the historical character the novel explicates the several layers of mystery through the social, religious and personal compulsions of violence. Nat emerges as a tragic hero who could almost say "Ripeness is all," as his life dramatizes fall from Grace by violence, and redemption through compassion.

IV

The dialectical tension between violence and compassion in *Nat Turner* converges in the murder of Margaret. While Nat wilfully chooses to shove compassion out of his heart as a sign of weakness and a symbol of obstruction in his cherished mission of emancipation from slavery, he also discerns in 'compassion' ultimately (through the brutal act of murdering Margaret) a force and a power to redeem him from monstrous violence. On the one hand, violence becomes necessary and inevitable to smash a cruel and inhuman system, and in this inexorable process, he has to become relentless on individuals who are integral to the system and uphold it. There is no quarter for mercy howsoever good and deserving the victim be. Otherwise the whole mission would crumble underneath the weight of misplaced goodness and kindness. The mission of achieving emancipation is divine even though the means employed to attain it are violent. And yet this antinomy between the means and ends—the way of achieving 'good' through 'evil'—strikes Nat, in the final analysis, as not an ideal way of gaining freedom. The murder of Margaret, in a sense, signifies the murder of humanity in man who cries out for a just order without the compulsive urge to massacre everyone who gets ranged and branded on the side of a tyrannous system. Is there no godly way to reach Godhead except through Satanic means? To establish a just order through humane methods? That is the dilemma plaguing a sensitive and humane rebel amidst the orgy of violence in the present times.

NOTES

1. Melvin J. Friedman and Irving Malin, *William Styron's The Confessions of Nat Turner: A Critical Handbook* (Belmont, Calif.: Wadsworth, Co., 1970), p. v.
2. Stanley Kaufmann, "Styron's Unwritten Novel," *Hudson Review*, 20, No. 4 (Winter 1967-68), p. 676.
3. Alan Holder, "Styron's Slave: *The Confessions of Nat Turner*," *South Atlantic Quarterly*, 68, No. 2 (Spring 1969), p. 180.

4. Wilfrid Sheed, "The Slave Who Became a Man", *The New York Times*, (8 October 1967), p. 2.
5. Richard Gilman, "Nat Turner Revisited", *The New Republic*, 27 April 1968, p. 24.
6. John H. Clarke, ed., *William Styron's "Nat Turner," Ten Black Writers Respond* (Boston: Beacon Press, 1968)
7. Ibid., p. v.
8. Ibid.
9. Ibid., p. viii.
10. Herbert Aptheker, "Styron's Turner Vs. Nat Turner," *New South Student*, 5 (May 1968), pp. 3-7.
11. Ibid.
12. John H. Clarke, p. viii.
13. R.W.B. Lewis and C. Vann Woodward, "Slavery in the First Person," *Yale Alumni Magazine*, November 1967. An Interview with William Styron, pp. 34-35.
14. George Plimpton, "William Styron: A Shared Ordeal", *The New York Times*, 8 October 1967. Interview with Styron, p. 2.
15. Thomas R. Gray, "The Confessions of Nat Turner", rpt. in Melvin J. Friedman and Irving Malin, eds. *The Confessions of Nat Turner: A Critical Handbook* p. 2.
16. Ibid., p. 14.
17. Ibid.
18. George Plimpton, pp. 36-42.
19. George Core, "*The Confessions of Nat Turner* and the Burden of the Past," *Southern Literary Journal*, Spring 1970; rpt. Robert K. Morris and Irving Malin, eds., *The Achievement of William Styron* (Athens: The Univ. of Georgia Press, 1975), p. 157.
20. Ibid., p. 165.
21. Ibid.
22. George Lukacs, *The Historical Novel*, trans. H. and S. Mitchell (London: The Merlin Press, 1962), p. 57.
23. William Styron, "Author's Note," *The Confessions of Nat Turner* (London: Jonathan Cape, 1968).

24. R.W.B. Lewis and C. Vann Woodward, p. 34.
25. George Lukacs, *The Historical Novel*, p. 58.
26. George Plimpton, p. 3.
27. Ibid.
28. Ibid., p. 2.
29. Ibid.
30. William Styron, "This Quiet Dust," *Harper's*, April 1965, pp. 135-46.
31. Ibid., p. 138.
32. R.W.B. Lewis and C. Vann Woodward, p. 39.
33. Ibid.
34. Page Stegner and Robert Conzoneri, "An Interview with William Styron", *Per/Se*, I (Summer 1969), pp. 37-44.
35. Ibid., p. 41.
36. Donald W. Markos, "Margaret Whitehead in *The Confessions of Nat Turner*," *Studies in the Novel*, 4, No. 1 (Spring 1972), p. 54.
37. Page Stegner and Robert Conzoneri, p. 42.
38. Ibid.
39. Donald W. Markos, p. 55.
40. Ibid.
41. George Plimpton, p. 34.

6

Conclusion

The preceding chapters of this study have explained Styron's creative use of his background and influences in his endeavour to unfold the post-war human predicament. Though he has projected violence as an inescapable fact of human existence, he is not content merely to analyse the causative factors of violence and brutality in the world. He has taken care to focus on its role in relation to suffering and compassion. A study of his novels will reveal his affirmative stance despite the violent and near-nihilistic predicament of the post-war world. The study, therefore, has been directed to evaluate Styron's allegiance to the Southern mode as well as the early influences on his art in the perspective of European tradition. Styron's relation to the Southern background becomes ambiguous by the fact that in spite of his disagreement with the regionalistic mode of criticism he has not rejected it totally as of no consequence. The ambiguity clearly points to the need to study the important elements in his work—the Southern, the Christian and the Existential—as converging in his tragic vision of man, especially in view of his informed awareness of the major fictional concerns of Europe chiefly France. The Southern background provides a vantage point to look at the human experience. The Christian and the Existential concerns in his work have helped Styron to consider "the spiritual aspects of life as significant in its own right." I have tried to go into the question of humanism and existentialism with reference to Camus in my analysis of Styron's vision and found the study fruitful. Styron has particularly valued Camus's "moral intensity." This is especially evident once we realise that Camus's tragic humanism rests on human solidarity inspired by compassion. David D. Galloway has referred to the concept of Camusian absurdity as relevant to Styron. He has, however, limited it to the conflict between "intention" and "reality." Styron in fact adopts Camus' moral intensity and not the pattern of situations to reveal the absurdity of human existence.

Styron has shown compassionate concern for the human beings at various levels—in absurd situations, in rebellion and in search of love and hope in a war-ridden world. He is very much involved in the celebration of human spirit in its confrontation with violence and despair. As man is driven to anonymity, the consequent psychic isolation necessitates violence as a means to affirm man's significance and establish a link between man and society. Though violence itself becomes a kind of communication, it often imperils community by its destructive force. It would become constructive when it is tempered by compassion which arises from the recognition of the community sense. Since violence brings man and community together ending man's hubristic isolation, it becomes a means of understanding and compassion as well. Violence erupts from man's attempt to affirm his existence. In the process, he understands the power of compassion through suffering.

Styron has exploited his Southern background to win insights into the role of violence in the evolution of human spirit, since the South has in a way become "the embodiment of violence in America." Styron appreciates the fictional concerns of the South as revealed in Faulkner's accent on "endurance," Warren's emphasis on self-discovery and O'Connor's religious predilections, and endows his characters with a tough moral fibre.

Styron's characters act violently, suffer, become compassionate and affirm the human values—hope, pity and love. Suffering as a cathartic act is completed in compassion antidoting hubristic isolation. One has to notice the meaningful interaction of violence and compassion qualifying Styron's tragic humanistic stance in the larger context of modern human predicament.

Styron's first novel *Lie Down in Darkness* has been often explained as another addition to Faulknerian pattern. The critical scholarship has combined Faulkner's pattern and the Southern tradition to detract from the original significance of Styron's novel. In fact, the South is only peripheral in the novel and although Faulkner's influence is not of the magnitude as has been made out in certain analyses by critics like Malcolm Cowley and John W. Aldridge, Styron has made use of Faulkner's complexity in solving the problem of time in his novel. *Lie Down in Darkness* reveals the failure of love and compassion and integrates the Southern background and psychological complexity of the characters to project the need of affirmation through compassion. The choral role of the Negroes Ruth and Ella Swan reveals the tragedy of the Loftis family in sharp contrast. Harry the Jew paints a portrait of hope in the midst of rubble suggesting the possibility of redemption even in the nihilistic void that has engulfed the Loftises. *Lie Down in Darkness* examines violence in its manifold destructive forms; Helen's soulless puritanism, Milton's self-defeating alcoholism and Peyton's masochistic nymphomania. Yet Styron evokes sympathy for Milton and Peyton very deftly creating the final impact as one of Christian compassion over Greek 'fate'. Styron's novel is a complex comment on endurance, faith and compassion—the human forces to counter the sterile secular existence of the Loftises.

Styron works out in detail the theme of protest as a human attribute in *The Long March*. Mannix the Jew vindicates his human worth only through protest which brings him great misery. The protest alone was the means to connect himself with the world outside, to affirm his humanity. Mannix's role has been often interpreted as born of *hubris*. The rebellious stance of Mannix is not hubris, and cannot be identified with 'sin' in the conventional Christian sense. Styron deliberately links Mannix with the line of mythic heroes to emphasize the tragic sense of life and its dignity born of integrity. Violence in *The Long March* leads the protagonist to the sources of compassion. Mannix can communicate with the Negro maid and admit his pain to her as both of them represent the two most highly persecuted races in human history. Violence and suffering have made them realise the power of compassion. Mannix has the moment of recognition in his encounter with the Negro maid. The Loftises cannot of course learn the life giving values from Ruth and Ella Swan. *The Long March* goes beyond *Lie Down in Darkness* in explicating the power of compassion.

Set This House on Fire dramatizes violence and compassion more powerfully than either of the earlier novels. Cass murders Mason Flagg inspired by his compassion for Michele, the dying Italian farmer, and his love for Francesca, the poor farmer's beautiful daughter. Luigi, the policeman prompts him to realise the positive aspects of life as he has himself experienced the demonic force of violence. The novel is a fable of tragic human lot revealing the transience of beauty, the inexplicability of violence and the unavailing compassion. Cass the protagonist in the end can only comment very uncertainly that he has somehow come to love 'being' instead of 'nothing,' at the end of his experience of depravity and terror.

The note of uncertainty regarding violence as a redeeming agent is no longer in *The Confessions of Nat Turner*. Nat's slavery, his betrayal by his masters, his compassion for his fellow slaves urge him to murder. Yet he realises the power of compassion through his only murder, as he kills Margaret Whitehead who has deeply loved him and treated as a human being. But in the life of Nat the act of murder becomes a redeeming factor with the realisation of his humanity. He gets beyond all the barriers and loves the Blacks and the whites as human beings. Nat finally feels that his God has come back to him—after his traumatic experience of desertion by God in the midst of violence and loss of humanity. The murder of Margaret has brought him face to face with the ultimate fact that he has to deal with real men and women and not abstract concepts. As he goes to the gallows he feels reconciled with God. He is uncontrite and yet he thinks that he would have spared Margaret. Styron has very subtly fused the social and the humanistic layers. As a rebel in a monstrous society, Nat had to kill. He is therefore uncontrite. As a human being the need to murder has revealed the significance of other human beings. The compassion for Margaret has made him reconsider his stance. The inevitable need of violence makes the human predicament tragic. Nat is portrayed in the novel as a sensitive human being—not merely a slave with his single minded urge to kill the whites. The terror of human tragedy is revealed further that in order to defend a set of valucs, the human agents resort to violence and in the end realise that by their violence they have destroyed the values. Violence exacts a heavy price in human terms. In a recent interview Styron has referred to the "tragic notion that men in revolutions destroy so much of the thing they love; namely they destroy their own notions of humanity by committing acts of violence against humanity. It's a paradox, it's totally unresolved and no revolution has ever been free of it."[1]

Styron's black critics have read the novel purely in a sociological context. *The Confessions of Nat Turner* is an effort in the direction of "humanising" an "insanely motivated religious fanatic."[2] It is unfair to Styron to read the novel as a historical document. The novel is in effect a culminating point in his efforts to validate in a literary form the dynamics of violence, suffering and compassion. In his four novels Styron has gradually progressed from the muted suggestion of the power of compassion in *Lie Down in Darkness*, through the meaningful encounter of the Jew and the Negro in *The Long March*, and also the conflict of violence and compassion in *Set This House on Fire* to the final assertion of violence—suffering compassion as a necessary redemptive nexus in the tragic history of Nat Turner. Styron's characters rebel in a dehumanised world to affirm their human worth and this results in violence. Violence and compassion are the invariable concomitants of tragic human existence. *The Confessions of Nat Turner* leaves the impression that Styron ultimately treats violence as a redemptive factor in his novels. He has told Ray Ownbey "maybe, after *Nat Turner* there is nothing left,"[3] in reply to the query about the further evolution of the theme after the violence of *Nat Turner*. *Sophie's Choice* is "in a curious way an extension of Nat Turner."[4]

NOTES

1. Ben Forkner and Gilbert Schricke, "An Interview with William Styron," *Southern Review*, 10, No. 4 (October 1974), p. 927.
2. Ibid., p. 925.
3. Ray Ownbey, "Discussions with William Styron," *The Mississippi Quarterly*, 30, No. 2 (Spring 1977), p. 293.
4. Ben Forkner and Gilbert Schricke, p. 929.

Bibliography

I. PRIMARY SOURCES

A. Novels:

Lie Down in Darkness. Indianapolis : Bobbs-Merrill, 1951; London: Hamish Hamilton, 1952; London: Jonathan Cape, 1970.

The Long March. New York: Random House, 1956; New York: Vintage, 1962; London: Hamish Hamilton, 1962.

Set This House on Fire. New York: Random House, 1960; London: Hamish Hamilton, 1962; London: Jonathan Cape, 1970.

The Confessions of Nat Turner, New York: Random House, 1967; London: Jonathan Cape, 1968.

Sophie's Choice. London: Jonathan Cape, 1979.

B. Play:

In the Clap Shack. New York: Random House, 1973.

C. Short Fiction:

"Autumn." In *One and Twenty: Duke Narrative and Verse, 1924-45*, edited by William M. Blackburn. Durham, N.C.: Duke University Press, 1945, pp. 36-53.

"The Long Dark Road." In *One and Twenty: Duke Narrative and Verse, 1924-45*, pp. 266-80. Reprinted in *William Styron's "The Confessions of Nat Turner"—A Critical Handbook*, edited by Melvin J. Friedman and Irving Malin. Belmont, Calif.: Wadsworth, 1970, pp. 116-25.

"A Moment in Trieste." In *American Vanguard*, edited by Don Wolfe. Ithaca, N.Y.: Cornell University Press, 1948. pp. 241-47. Reprinted in *New Voices: American Writing Today*, edited by Don Wolfe. Garden City, N.Y.: Doubleday, 1953.

"The Enormous Window." In *1950 American Vanguard*, edited by Charles I, Glicksberg. New York: School for Social Research, 1950, pp. 71-89.

"The Long March." In *Discovery No. 1*, edited by John W. Aldridge and Vance Bourjail. New York: Pocket Books, 1953, pp. 221-83. Collected as L.M. Reprinted in *The Best Short Stories of World War II: An American Anthology*, edited by Charles Fenton. New York: Viking Press, 1957, pp. 361-421.

"The McCabes." *Paris Review*, 22 (Autumn-Winter 1959-60): pp. 12-28. Incorporated into SHF.

"Works in Progress." *Esquire* 60 (July 1963), 50-51, 105. Incorporated into N T.

"Runaway." *Partisan Review*, 32 (Fall 1966), pp. 574-82.

"Virginia: 1931." *Paris Review*, 9 (Winter 1966), pp. 13-45. Incorporated into NT.

"The Confessions of Nat Turner." *Harper's*, 235 (September 1967), pp. 51-102. Incorporated into NT.

"Novel's Climax: The Night of the Honed Axes." *Life*, 63 (13 October 1967), pp. 54-60. Incorporated into NT.

"Marriott, the Marine." *Esquire*, 76 (September 1971), pp. 101-04, 196, 198, 200, 202, 204, 207, 208, 210.

D. Articles:

"Letters to an Editor." *Paris Review*, 1 (Spring 1953), pp. 9-16,

"Prevalence of Wonders." *Nation*, 176 (2 May 1953), pp. 370-71.

"The Paris Review." *Harper's Bazaar*, 87 (August 1953), pp. 122-73.

"What's Wrong with the American Novel?" *American Scholar*, 24 (Autumn 1955), pp. 464-503. [Round table discussion with Ralph Ellison, Hiram Haydn, and others.]

"If You Write for Television. . . ." *New Republic*, 146 (6 April 1959), p. 16.

Introduction to *Best Short Stories from "The Paris Review."* New York: E.P. Dutton, 1959, pp. 9-16.

"Mrs. Aadland's Little Girl, Beverly." *Esquire* (November 1961); pp. 142, 189-91. Reprinted in *First Person Singular: Essays for the Sixties*, edited by Herbert Gold. New York: Dial Press, 1963, pp. 209-16. Reprinted in *Esquire's World of Humor*. New York: Esquire, 1964, p. 210 [as "True Confessions"].

"The Death-in-Life of Benjamin Reid." *Esquire*, 57 (February 1962), pp. 114, 141-45. Reprinted in *An Approach to Literature*, edited by Cleanth Brooks, John Thibaut Purser, and Robert Penn Warren. 4th ed. New York: Appleton-Century-Crofts, 1964, pp. 496-503.

"As He Lay Dead, A Bitter Grief." *Life*, 53 (20 July 1962), pp. 39-42.

"Aftermath of Benjamin Reid." *Esquire*, 58 (November 1962), p. 79.

"Writers under Twenty-five." In *Under Twenty-five: Duke Narrative and Verse, 1945-62*, edited by William M. Blackburn. Durham, N.C.: Duke University Press, 1963, pp. 3-8.

"Two Writers Talk It Over." *Esquire*, 60 (July 1963); 57-59. [Discussion with James Jones.]

"This Quiet Dust." *Harper's*, 230 (April 1965), pp. 135-46. Reprinted in *Best Magazine Articles of the Year 1966*, edited by Gerald Walker. New York: Crown Publishers, 1966, pp. 1-18. Reprinted in *William Styron's "The Confessions of Nat*

Turner"—a Critical Handbook, edited by Friedman and Malin (See 1, C above), pp. 18-35.

"Truth and Nat Turner: An Exchange—William Styron Replies." *Nation*, 206 (22 April 1968), pp. 544-47.

"Oldest America." *McCalls*, 95 (July 1968), pp. 94, 1 23.

"Symposium: Violence in Literature." *American Scholar*, 37 (Summer 1968), pp. 482-496. (Round table with Robert Penn Warren, Theodore Solotaroff, and Robert Coles).

"In the Jungle." *New York Review of Books*, 11 (26 September 1968), pp. 11-13.

"My Generation." *Esquire*, 70 (October 1968), pp. 123-24.

"On Creativity." *Playboy*, 15 (December 1968). (Styron's statement appears on p. 138.)

"The Uses of Historical Fiction." *Southern Literary Journal*, 1 (Spring 1969), pp. 57-90. (Discussion with Ralph Ellison, Robert Penn Warren, C. Vann Woodward, and Styron.)

"Kuznetcov's Confession." *New York Times*, 14 September 1969, sec. 4, p. 13. (Letter to the editor clarifying Styron's position on Kuznetsov's defection.)

"A Letter from William Styron." *Barat Review*, 6 (Spring/-Summer 1971), p. 5.

"Reflections." *Ploughshares*, 1, No. 3 (1972), pp. 82-84.

E. Book and Record Reviews:

"New Editions." *New York Review of Books*, 1 (Special issue 1963), p. 43. (*Slave and Citizen: The Negro in the Americas* by Frank Tannonbaum).

"Overcome." *New York Review of Books*, 1 (26 September 1963), pp. 18-19. (*American Negro Slave Revolts* by Herbert Aptheker).

"An Elegy for F. Scott Fitzgerald." *New York Review of Books* 1 (28 November 1963), pp. 1-13. (*The Letters of F. Scott Fitzgerald*, edited by Andrew Turnbull).

"The Habit." *New York Review of Books*, 1 (26 December 1963), pp. 13-14. (*The Consumers Union Report on Smoking and the Public Interest*, edited by Ruth and Bdward Brecher).

"A Southern Conscience." *New York Review of Books*, 2 (2 April 1964), p. 3. (*A Southern Prophecy* by Lewis H. Blair).

"Tootsie Rolls." *New York Review of Books*, 2 (14 May 1964), pp. 8-9. (*Candy* by Terry Southern and Mason Hoffenberg).

"MacArthur." *New York Review of Books*, 2 (8 October 1964), pp. 3-5. (*Reminiscences* by Douglas MacArthur).

"John Fitzgerald Kennedy . . . as we remember him." *High Fidelity*, 16 (January 1966),p. 38. ("John Fitzgerald Kennedy . . . as we remember him" by Charles Kuralt: Columbia Recording L2L: 1017).

"The Vice That Has No Name." *Harper's* 236 (February, 1968), pp. 97-100. (*Light on Dark Corners . . .* by B.G. Jefferis and J.L. Nichols).

"The Shade of Thomas Wolfe." *Harper's*, 236 (April 1968), pp. 96, 98-104. (*Thomas Wolfe* by Andrew Turnbull).

"A Timeless, Walled Yaddo for Gifted Misfit." *New York Times Book Review*, 25 April 1971, pp. 1, 10, 12. (The Joint by James Blake).

"That Extraordinary Company of Writers Ironically Known as the Lost Generation." *New York Times Book Review*, 6 May 1973, pp. 8. 10, 12, 14. (*A Second Flowering* by Malcolm Cowley).

II. SECONDARY SOURCES

A. Books:

Aldridge, John W. "The Society of Three Novels." In his *In Search of Heresy*. New York: McGraw-Hill, 1956, pp. 126-48 (LDD)

. "William Styron and the Derivative Imagination." In his *Time to Murder and Create: The Contemporary Novel in Crisis*. New York: David McKay, 1966, pp. 30-51. (SHF)

Allen, Walter. *The Modern Novel in Britain and the United States*. New York: E.P. Dutton, 1964, pp. 305-07. (LDD)

——. *Tradition and Dream: The English and American Novel From the Twenties to Our Time.* London: J.M. Dent, 1974.

Baumbach, Jonathan. "Paradise Lost: *Lie Down in Darkness* by William Styron." In his *The Landscape of Nightmare: Studies in the Contemporary Novel.* New York: New York University Press, 1965, pp. 123-37.

Bradbury, John M. *Renaissance in the South: A Critical History of the Literature, 1920-60.* Chapel Hill: University of North Carolina Press, 1963, pp. 122-23 and passim. (LDD and SHF)

Bryant, Jerry H. *The Open Decision—The Contemporary American Novel and its Intellectual Background.* New York: Free Press, 1970, pp. 264-68. (SHF)

Bryer, Jackson and Hatem, Mary B. William. *Styron: A Reference Guide.* Reference Publications Service, 1978.

Butor, Michel. *Preface to La Proie des flammes.* Translated by M.E. Coindreuu. Paris: Gallimard, 1963, pp. vii-xx.

Clarke, John H., ed. *William Styron's "Nat Turner": Ten Black Writers Respond.* Boston: Beacon Press, 1968.

Core, George, ed. *Southern Fiction Today: Renascence and Beyond.* Athens: University of Georgia Press, 1969.

Cowley, Malcolm. *Writers at Work: 'The Paris Review' Interview.* London: Mercury Books, 1962.

Davis, Robert Gorham. "The American Individualist Tradition: Bellow and Styron." In *The Creative Present: Notes on Contemporary Fiction,* edited by Nona Balakian and Charles Simmons. Garden City, N. Y.: Doubleday, 1963, pp. 111-41.

Detweiler, Robert. "William Styron and the Courage to Be." In his *Four Spiritual Crises in Mid-Century American Fiction.* Gainesville: University of Florida Press, 1964, pp. 6-13.

Duberman, Martin. "William Styron's *Nat Turner and Ten Black Writers Respond.*" In his *The Uncompleted Past.* New York: Random House, 1969, pp. 203-22. (Reprinted reviews plus new "second thoughts" on both pieces).

Duff, John B. and Mitchell, Peter M., ed. *The Nat Turner Rebellion: The Historical Event and the Modern Controversy.* New York: Harper and Row, 1971.

Finkelstein, Sidney. "Cold War, Religious Revival, and Family Alienation: William Styron, J.D. Salinger, and Edward Albee." In his *Existentialism and Alienation in American Literature.* New York: International Publishers, 1965, pp. 211-242.

Foner, Eric. *Nat Turner.* Englewood Cliffs, N.J.: Prentice-Hall, 1971.

Fossum, Robert H. *William Styron: A Critical Essay.* Grand Rapids, Mich.: Berdmans, 1968.

Friedman, Melvin J. "William Styron." In *The Politics of Twentith-Century Novelists,* edited by George A. Panichas. New York: Hawthorn Books, 1971, pp. 335-50.

——, and Irving Malin, eds. *William Styron's "The Confessions of Nat Turner—A Critical Handbook,* Belmont, Calif.: Wadsworth, 1970.

——, and Angust J. Nigro, eds. *Configuration critique de William Styron.* Paris: Minard, 1967.

Galloway, David D. "The Absurd Man as Tragic Hero" and "A William Styron Checklist." In his *The Absurd Hero in American Fiction.* Austin University of Taxes Press, 1966, pp. 51-80 and 203-10.

Geismar, Maxwell. "William Styron: The End of Innocence." In his *Americn Moderns : From Rebellion to Conformity.* New York: Hill and Wang, 1958. pp. 239-50.

Gossett, Louise Y. "The Cost of Freedom: William Styron." In her *Violence in Recent Southern Fiction.* Durham, N.C.: Duke University Press, 1965, pp. 117-30.

Hartt, Julian. *The Lost Image of Man.* Baton Rouge: Louisiana State University Press, 1963, pp. 60-63, 130.

Hassan, Ihab. "Encounter with Necessity: Three Novels by Styron, Swados, and Mailer." In his *Radical Innocence: Studies in the Contemporary American Novel.* Princeton, N.J.: Princeton University Press, 1961, pp. 124-52. (LDD) Reprinted in *On Contemporary Literature,* edited by

Richard Kostelanetz. New York: Avon. 1964, Pp. 597-606; and in *William Styron's "The Confessions of Nat Turner."—A Critical Handbook*, edited by Friedman and Malin, pp. 141-148.

Hoffman, Frederick J. "The Sense of Place." In *South: Modern Southern Literature in its Cultural Setting*, edited by Louis D. Rubin, Jr. and Robert D. Jacobs. Garden City, N. Y.: Doubleday Dolphin, 1961, pp. 76-94. (LDD)

——. "William Styron: The Metaphysical Hurt." In his *The Art of Southern Fiction: A Study of Some Modern Novelists*. Carbondale: Southern Illinois University Press, 1967, pp. 144-161. Reprinted in *Configuration critique de William Styron*, edited by Friedman and Nigro (see above), pp. 33-56 (in French); and in *William Styron's "The Confessions of Nat Turner"—A Critical Handbook*, edited by Friedman and Malin, pp. 126-41.

Kaufmann, Walter. *Tragedy and Philosophy*. Garden City, N. Y.: Doubleday, 1969.

Kazin, Alfred. "The Alone Generation." In his *Contemporaries*. Boston: Little, Brown, 1962, pp. 214-16.

Kort, Wesley A. "*The Confessions of Nat Turner* and the Dynamic Revolution." In his *Shriven Selves—Religious Problems in Recent American Fiction*. Philadelphia: Fortress Press, 1972, pp. 116-49.

Kostelanetz, Richard. *On Contemporary Literature*. New York: Avon Books, 1964.

Kuehl, John. Appendix to his *Write and Rewrite—A Study of the Creative Process*. New York: Meredith Press, 1967, pp. 294-308. *Write and Rewrite* was also published under the title *Creative Writing and Rewriting* by Appleton-Century-Crofts. (Facsimile of Styron's holograph of Chap. 1 of LM and the published version).

Lawson, Lewis A. "William Styron (1925-)." In *A Bibliographical Guide to the Study of Southern Literature*, edited by Louis D. Rubin, Jr. Baton Rouge: Louisiana State Univ. Press, 1969, pp. 300-02. (Selective and unannotated list of secondary materials.)

Ludwig, Jack. *Recent American Novelists*. Minneapolis: University of Minnesota Press, 1962, pp. 31-34.

Mackin, Cooper R. *William Styron.* Austin, Tex: Steck-Vaughn, 1969.

Mailer, Norman. *Advertisements for Myself.* New York: New American Library, 1960, Pp. 415-16.

Matthiessen, Peter, and Plimpton, George. "William Styron." In *Writers at Work: The "Paris Review" Interviews*, edited by Malcolm Cowley. New York: Viking Press, 1959, pp. 267-82.

Morris, Robert K. and Irving Malin, eds. *The Achievement of William Styron.* Athens: The University of Georgia Press, 1975.

Mudrick, Marvin. "Mailer and Styron." In his *On Culture and Literature.* New York: Horizon Press, 1970, pp. 176-99.

O'Connor, William Van. "John Updike and William Styron: The Burden of Talent." In *Contemporary American Novelists*, edited by Harry T. Moore. Carbondale: Southern Illinois University Press, 1964, pp. 205-21.

Pearce, Richard. *William Styron.* Minneapolis: University of Minnesota Press, 1971.

Ratner, Marc L. *William Styron.* New York: Twayne. 1972.

Rubin, Louis D., Jr. *The Curious Death of the Novel: Essays in American Literature.* Baton Rouge: Louisiana State University Press, 1967, pp. 4, 9, 10, 20-22, 146-47, 277, 280, 286, 292.

———. "William Styron: Notes on a Southern Writer in Our Time." In his *The Faraway Country: Writers of the Modern South.* Seattle: University of Washington Press, 1963, pp. 185-230.

——. Porter, Katherine Anne: O'Connor, Flannery: Gordon, Caroline; and Jones, Madison. *Recent Southern Finction.* Macon, Ga.: Wesleyan College, 1960.

Stevenson, David L. "Novelists of Distinction." In *The Creative Present*, edited by Nona Balakian and Charles Simmons. Garden City. N. Y.: Doubleday, 1963, pp. 195-212.

——. "William Styron and the Fiction of the Fifties." In *Recent American Fiction: Some Critical Views*, edited by Joseph L. Waldmeir. Boston: Houghton Mifflin, 1963, pp. 265-274.

Tischler, Nancy M. *Black Masks: Negro Characters in Modern Southern Fiction*. London: The Pennsylvania State Univ. Press, 1969.

Urang, Gunnar. "The Voices of Tragedy in the Novels of William Styron." In *Adversity and Grace: Studies in Recent American Literature*, edited by Nathan A, Scott, Jr. Chicago: University of Chicago Press. 1968, pp. 183-209.

West, James L. *William Styron: A Descriptive Bibliography*. New York: Reference Publications Service, 1977.

"William Styron." In *A Library of Literary Criticism: Modern American Literature*, edited by Dorothy Hyren. New York: Frederick Ungar, 1960, pp. 473-76.

B. Periodicals:

Akin, William E. "Toward an Impressionistic History: Pitfalls and Possibilities in William Styron's Meditation on History." *American Quarterly*, 21 (Winter 1969), pp. 805-12.

Aldridge, John W. "Highbrow Authors and Middlebrow Books." *Playboy*, 11 (April 1964), pp. 173-74.

Amis, Harry D. "History as Self-serving Myth: Another Look at Styron's *The Confessions of Nat Turner*." *The College Language Association Journal*, 22, No. 2 (December 1978)

Aptheker, Herbert. "A Note on the History." *Nation*, 205 (16 October 1967), pp. 375-76.

Arms, Valerie Meliotes. "An Interview with William Styron," *Contemporary Literature*, 20, 1 (1979), pp. 1-12.

Baker, John. "William Styron" in *Conversations with Writers. II*. Detroit: Gale, pp. 257-82.

Barzelay, Douglas, and Robert Gussman. "William Styron on *The Confessions of Nat Turner*: A Yale Lit. Interview." *Yale Literary Magazine*, 137 (September 1968), pp. 24-35.

Baumbach, Jonathan. "Paradise Lost: The Novels of William Styron." *South Atlantic Quarterly*, 63 (Spring 1964), pp. 207-17. Reprinted in his *The Landscape of Nightmare*.

Bennett, Lerone, Jr. "The Case against Styron's Nat Turner." *Ebony*, 23 (October 1968), pp. 148-50, 154-57.

Benson, Alice R. "Techniques in the Twentieth Century Novel for Relating the Particular to the Universal: *Set This House on Fire*." *Papers of the Michigan Academy of Science, Arts, and Letters*, 47 (1962), pp. 587-94.

"Biographical Sketches of Persons Selected for the Pulitzer Prizes for 1968." *New York Times*, 7 May 1968, p. 34.

Bonnichon, Anre. "William Styron et le second oedipe." *Etudes*, 315 (October 1962), pp. 94-103. (SHF)

Borders, William. "M'Carthy Gaining in Connecticut." *New York Times*, 10 March 1968, p. 46. (Styron was a delegate to the Democratic Convention.)

Brandriff, Welles T. "The Role of Order and Disorder in *The Long March*." *English Journal*, 56 (January 1967), pp. 54-59.

Brunaur, Dalma H. "Black and White: The Archetypal Myth and Its Development." *Barat Review*, 6 (Spring/Summer 1971), pp. 12-19.

Bryant, Jerry H. "The Hopeful Stoicism of William Styron." *South Atlantic Quarterly*, 62 (Autumn 1963), pp. 539-550.

Cannon, Patricia R. "Nat Turner: God, Man, or Beast ?" *Barat Review*, 6 (Spring/Summer 1971), pp. 25-28.

Canzoneri, Robert, and Page Stenger. "An Interview with William Styron." *Per/se*, 1 (Summer 1966), pp. 37-44.

Cheshire, Ardner R., Jr. "The Recollective Structure of *The Confessions of Nat Turner*." *Southern Review*, 12, (1976), pp. 110-21.

Cheyer, A.H. "WLB Biography: William Styron." *Wilson Library Bulletin*, 36 (April 1962), p. 691.

Cooke, Michael. "Nat Turner: Another Response." *Yale Review*, 58 (Winter 1960), pp. 295-301 (Review of Clarke's *William Styron's "Nat Turner*.")

Core, George. "*The Confessions of Nat Turner* and the Burden of the Past." *Southern Literary Journal*, 2 (Spring 1970), pp. 117-34.

——. "Nat Turner and the Final Reckoning of Things." *Southern Review*, 4 (Summar 1968), pp. 745-51.

Curtis, Bruce. "Fiction, Myth, and History in William Styron's *Nat Turner*." *University College Quarterly*, 16 (January 1971), pp. 27-32.

Davis, Robert Gorham. "Styron and the Students." *Critique*, 3 (Summer 1960), pp. 37-46.

Dempsey, David. "Talk with William Styron." *New York Times Book Review*, 9 September 1951, p. 27.

Doar, Harriet. "Interview with William Styron." *Red Clay Reader*, 1964, pp. 26-30.

Duberman, Martin. "Historical Fictions." *New York Times Book Review*, 11 August 1968, pp. 1, 26-27. (Review of Clarke's *William Styron's 'Nat Turner'*).

Durden, Robert F. "William Styron and His Black Critics." *South Atlantic Quarterly*, 68 (Spring 1969), pp. 181-87. (Review of Clarke's *William Styron's 'Nat Turner*.')

Firestone, Bruce M. "A Rose is a Rose is a Columbine: *Citizen Kane* and William Styron's *Nat Turner*." *Literature/Film Quarterly*, 5 pp. 118-24.

Flanders, Jane. "William Styron's Southern Myth." *Louisiana Studies*, 15, pp. 263-78.

Foster, Richard. "An Orgy of Commerce: William Styron's *Set This House on Fire*." *Critique*, 3 (Summer 1960), pp. 59-70.

Franklin, Jimme L. "Nat Turner and Black History." *Indian Journal of American Studies*, 1 (November 1971), pp. 1-6.

Friedman, Melvin J. "The Cracked Vase." *Romance Notes*, 7 (Spring 1966), pp. 127-29.

Fuentes, Carols. "Unslavish Fidelity." *Times Literary Supplement* (London), 16 May 1968, p. 505.

Galloway, David D. "The Absurd Man as Tragic Hero: The Novels of William Styron." *Texas Studies in Literature and Language*, 6 (Winter 1965), pp. 512-34. Reprinted in his *The Absurd Hero in American Fiction*.

Geismar, Maxwell. "The American Short Story Today." *Studies on the Left*, 4 (Spring 1964), pp. 21-27.

Genovese, Eugene D. "An Exchange on '*Nat Turner*'." *New York Review of Books*, 11 (7 November 1968), pp. 34-36.

———. "The Nat Turner Case." *New York Review of Books*, 11 (12 September 1968), pp. 34-37. (Review of Clarke's *William Styron's 'Nat Turner*.')

Gilman, Richard. "Nat Turner Revisited." *New Republic*, 158 (27 April 1968), pp. 23-32. Reprinted in William Styron's "*The Confessions of Nat Turner*"—*A Critical Handbook*, edited by Friedman and Malin.

Gray, Richard. "Victims and History and Agents of Revolution: An Approach to William Styron." *Dutch Quarterly Review of Anglo-American Letters*, 5, pp. 3-23.

Gross, Seymour L. and Eileen Bender. "History and Politics, and Literature: The Myth of Nat Turner.', *American Quarterly*, 23 (October 1971) pp. 486-518.

H., E.P. "On Author." *Saturday Review of Literature*, 34 (15 September 1951), p. 12.

Hamilton, Charles V. "Nat Turner Reconsidered: The Fiction and the Reality." *Saturday Review*, 51 (22 June 1968), pp. 22-23. (Review of Clarke's *William Styron's 'Nat Turner*.')

Harding, Vincent. "An Exchange on 'Nat Turner." *New York Review of Books*, 11 (7 November 1968), pp. 31-33.

Hassan, Ihab. "The Character of Post-War Fiction in America." *English Journal*, 51 (January 1962), pp. 1-8.

———. "The Novel of Outrage: A Minority Voice in Postwar American Fiction." *American Scholar*, 34 (Spring 1965), pp. 239-53 (243-44).

Hays, Peter L. "The Nature of Rebellion in *The Long March*." *Critique*, 7 (Winter 1965-66), pp. 70-74.

Hazard, E.P. "Eight Fiction Finds." *Saturday Review of Literature*, 35 (16 February 1952), p. 17.

———. "William Styron." *Saturday Review of Literature*, 34 (15 September 1951), p. 12.

Holder, Alan. "Styron's Slave *The Confessions of Nat Turner*." *South Atlantic Quarterly*, 68 (Spring 1969), pp. 167-80.

Hutchens, John K. "William Styron." *New York Herald Tribune Book Review*, 9 September 1951, p. 2.

Kazin, Alfred. "The Alone Generation." *Harper's* (Special Supplement), 219 (October 1959), pp. 127-31. Reprinted in his *Contemporaries*.

Klotz, Marvin. "The Triumph Over Time: Narrative Form in William Faulkner and William Styron." *Mississippi Quarterly*, 17 (Winter 1964-64), pp. 9-20.

Kostelanetz, Richard. "The Bad Criticism of this Age." *Minnesota Review*, 4 (Spiring 1964), pp. 389-414.

Lawson, John Howard. "William Styron: Darkness and Fire in the Modern Novel." *Mainstream*, 13 (October 1960), pp. 9-18. (SHF)

Lawson, Lewis. "Cass Kinsolving : Kierkegaardian Man of Despair." *Wisconsin Studies in Contemporary Literature*, 3 (Fall 1962), pp. 54-60.

Leo, John. "Some Negroes Accuse Styron of Distorting Nat Turner's Life." *New York Times*, 1 February 1968, p. 34.

Lewis, R.W.B. and C. Vann Woodward. "Slavery in the First Person." *Yale Alumni Magazine*, 31 (November 1967), pp. 33-39.
(Interview about NT.) Reprinted in *William Styron's "The Confessions of Nat Turner"—A Critical Handbook*, edited by Friedman and Malin.

McNamara, Eugene. "The Post-Modern American Novel." *Queen's Quarterly*, 69 (Summer 1962), pp. 265-75.

Mailer, Norman. "Norman Mailer vs. Nine Writers." *Esquire*, 60 (July 1963), pp. 63-69, 105.

Markos, Donald W. "Margaret Whitehead in *The Confessions of Nat Turner*." *Studies in the Novel*, 4 (Spring 1972), pp. 52-59.

Matthiessen, Peter, and George Plimpton. "William Styron." *Paris Review*, 5 (Spring 1954), pp. 42-47. (Interview.) Reprinted in *Writers at Work*, edited by Cowley.

Meras, Phyllis. "The Author." *Saturday Review*, 50 (October 1967), p. 30.

Mitchell, Morse J. "Social Relevance, Literary Judgement and the New Right: Or. The Inadvertent Confessions of William Styron." *College English*, 30 (1969), pp. 605-16.

Moore, L. Hugh. "Robert Penn Warren, William Styron, and the Use of Greek Myth." *Critique*, 8 (Winter 1965-66), pp. 75-87.

Morse, J. Mitchell. "Social Relevance, Literary Judgment and the New Right: or, The Inadvertent Confessions of William Styron." *College English*, 30 (May 1969), pp. 605-16 pp. 614-615: NT).

Mudrick, Marvin. "Mailer and Styron: Guests of the Establishment." *Hudson Review*, 17 (Autumn 1964), pp. 346-66.

Mullen, Jean S. "Styron's Nat Turner: A Search for Humanity." *Barat Review*, 6 (Spring/Summer 1971), pp. 6-11.

Nigro, August. "*The Long March*. The Expansive Hero in a Closed World." *Critique*, 9, No. 3 (1967), pp. 103-12.

Noggle, Burt. "Variety and Ambiguity." *Mississippi Quarterly*, 17 (Winter 1963-64), p. 33.

Nolte, William H. "Styron's Meditation on Saviors." *Southwest Review*, 58 (Autumn 1973), pp. 338-48.

O'Connell, Shaum. "Expense of Spirit: The Vision of William Styron." *Critique*, 8 (Winter 1965-68), pp. 20-33.

Ownbey, Ray. "Discussions with William Styron." *Mississippi Quarterly*, 30 (Spring 1977), pp. 283-95.

Perry, J. Douglas, Jr. "Gothic as Vortex: The Form of Terror in Capote, Faulkner, and Styron." *Modern Fiction Studies*, 19, pp. 153-57.

Plimpton, George. "William Styron: A Shared Ordeal." *New York Times Book Review*, 8 October 1967, pp. 2, 3, 30, 32, 34.

Ratner, Marc L. "Rebellion of Wrath and Laughter: Styron's *Set This House on Fire*." *Southern Review*, 7 (Autumn 1971), pp. 1007-1020.

——. "The Rebel Purged: Styron's *The Long March*." *Arlington Quarterly*, 2 (Autumn 1969), pp. 27-42.

———. "Styron's Rebel." *American Quarterly*, 21 (Fall 1969), 595-608.

Robb, Kenneth A. "William Styron's Don Juan." *Critique*, 8 (Winter 1965-66), pp. 34-46.

Roth, Philip. "Writing American Fiction." *Commentary*, 31 (March 1961), pp. 223-33 (p. 232).

Rubin, Louis, D., Jr., "Notes on the Literary Scene: Their Southerners' Own Language." *Harper's*, 230 (April 1965), pp. 173-75.

Schneider, Harold W. "Two Bibliographies: Saul Bellow, William Styron." *Critique*, 3 (Summer 1960), pp. 71-91.

Shapiro, Herbert. "The Confessions of Nat Turner: William Styron and His Critics." *Negro American Literature Forum*, 9, pp. 99-104.

Stevenson, David L. "Styron and the Fiction of the Fifties." *Crittque*, 3 (Summer 1960), pp. 47-58. Reprinted in *Recent American Fiction*, edited by Waldmeir.

Suter, Anthony. Transcendence and Failure: William Styron's *Lie Down in Darkness*." *Caliban*, 12 (1975), pp. 157-66.

Swanson, William J. "Religious Implications in *The Confessions of Nat Turner*." *Cimarron Review*, No. 12 (July 1970), pp. 57-66.

Thelwell, Michael. "Arguments: The Turner Thesis." *Partisan Review*, 35 (Summer 1968), pp. 403-412; reply by Robert Coles, pp. 412-14.

———. "An Exchange on 'Nat Turner'", *New York Review of Books*, 11 (6 November 1968), p. 34.

———. "Mr. William Styron and the Rev. Turner." *Massachusetts Review*, 9 (Winter 1961), pp. 7-28. Reprinted in *William Styron's 'Nat Turner*,' edited by Clarke.

Thorp, Willard. "The Southern Mode." *South Atlantic Quarterly*, 63 (Autumn 1964), pp. 576-582 pp. 578-79).

"The Times Diary." *Times* (London), 2 April 1969, p. 10. (On controversy over filming of NT.)

Times Literary Supplement (London), 5 August 1955, pp. ii-iii.

Tischler, Nancy M. "*The Confessions of Nat Turner*: A Symposium—Introducton." *Barat Review*, 6 (Spring/Summer 1971), pp. 3-4.

——. "Negro Literature and Classic Form." *Contemporary Literature*, 10 (Summer 1969), pp. 352-65. (NT and Invisible man.

Trocard, Catherine. "William Styron and the Historical Novel, *Neohelicon*. 3, pp. i-ii, 373-82.

Urang, Gunnar. "The Broader Vision: William Styron's *Set This House on Fire.*" *Critique*, 8 (Winter 1965-66), pp. 47-69.

Waldmeir, Joseph. "Quest without Faith." *Nation*, 193 (18 November 1961), pp. 390-96.

Wells, Anna Mary. "An Exchange on 'Nat Turner.' "*New York Review of Books*, 11 (7 November 1968), p. 31.

West, James L. W. III. "A Bibliographer's Interview with William Styron." *Costerus*, 4, pp. 13-29.

——"William Styron's Afterword to *The Long March*," *Mississippi Quarterly*, 28, pp. 185-89.

White, John. "The Novelist as Historian: William Styron and American Negro Slavery." *Journal of American Studies, 4* (February 1971), pp. 233-45.

Winner, Anthony. "Adjustment, Tragic Humanism, and Italy." *Studi Americani*, 7 (1961), pp. 311-61.

Zipper Cunod Roberta. "An Anamoly of 'and'."*Linguistics in Literature*, 2, ii, pp. 19-42.

C. Doctoral Dissertations:

Arms, Valarie Meliotes. "William Styron's Literary Career." Temple University, 1977.

Baumbach, Jonathan. "The Theme of Guilt and Redemption in the Post Second World War Novel." Stanford University, 1961.

Cheshire, Ardner R., Jr. "The Theme of Redemption in the Fiction of William Styron." The Louisiana State University and Agricultural and Mechanical College, 1973.

Corodimas Peter N. "Guilt and Redemption in the Novels of William Styron." Ohio State University, 1971.

Galloway, David. D. "The Absurd Hero in Contemporary Fiction: The works of John Updike, William Styron, Saul Bellow, and J. D. Salinger." University of Buffalo, 1962.

Firestone, Bruce Michael. "A Study of William Styron's Fiction." The University of North Carolina, 1975.

Goodley, Nancy Carter. "All Flesh in Grass: Despair and Affirmation in *Lie Down in Darkness.*" The American University, 1975.

Hux, Samuel H. "American Myth and Existential Vision: The Indigenous Existentialism of Mailer, Bellow, Styron, and Ellison." University of Connecticut, 1966.

Kime, Benna K. "A Critical Study of the Technique of William Styron." Tulane University, 1971.

Lang, John Douglas. *William Styron: The Christian Imagination* Stanford Uuiversity, 1975.

Luttrell, William. "Tragic and Comic Modes in Twentieth Century American Literature: William Styron and Joseph Heller." Bowling Green State University, 1969.

Mewshaw, Michael F. "Thematic and Stylistic Problems in the Work of William Styron." University of Virginia, 1970.

Mills, Eva Bamberger. "The Development of William Styron's Artistic Consciousness: A Study of the Relationship Between Life and Work." University of Cincinnato, 1976.

Morgan, Henry G., Jr. "The World as Prison: A Study of the Novels of William Styron." University of Colorado, 1972.

Nelson, Doris L. "The Contemporary American Family Novel: A Study of Metaphor." University of Southern California, 1970.

Nigro, August. "William Styron and the Adamic Tradition. University of Maryland, 1964.

O'Connell, Shaun V. "The Contexts of William Styron's *The Confessions of Nat Turner.*" University of Massachusetts, 1970.

Ownbey, Ray W. "To Choose Being: The Function of Order and Disorder in William Styron's Fiction." University of Utah, 1972.

Peterson, Sandra M. "The View from the Gallows: The Criminal Confession in American Literature." North-Western University, 1972,

Scott, James B. " The Individual and Society: Norman Mailer versus William Styron." Syracuse University, 1964.

Swanson, William J. "William Styron: Eloquent Protestant." Northern Colorado University, 1972.

D. Book Reviews:

Lie Down in Darkness

Aldridge, John W. "In a Place Where Love Is a Stranger." *New York Times Book Review*, 9 Spetember 1951, p. 5.

Breit, Harvey. "Dissolution of a Family." *Atlantic Monthly*, 188 (October 1951), pp. 78-80.

Chapin, Ruth. "Twilight of the South. *Christian Science Monitor*, 4 October 1951, p. 11.

Cowley, Malcolm. "The Faulkner pattern." *New Republic*, 125 (8 October 1951), pp. 19-20.

"Dark Misery. *Newsweek*, 38 (10 September 1951), pp. 106-7.

Davis, Robert Gorham. "A Grasp of Moral Realities." *American Scholar*, 21 (Winter 1951-52), pp. 114, 116.

Downing, Francis. "The Young: A Lost Generation." *Commonweal*, 54 (5 October 1951), p. 620.

Geismar, Maxwell. "Domestic Tragedy in Virginia." *Saturday Review of Literature*, 34 (15 September 1941), pp. 12-13.

Janeway, Elizabeth. "Private Emotion Privately Felt." *New Leader*, 35 (21 January 1952), p. 25.

Jones, Howard Mumford. "A Rich, Moving Novel Introduces a Young Writer of Great Talent." *New York Herald Tribune Book Review*, 9 September 1951, p. 3.

Kirby, John Pendy. *Virginia Quarterly Review*. 28 (Winter 1952) pp. 129-30.

New Yorker, 27 (20 September 1951), pp. 118-19.

O'Brien, Alfred. Jr. "Lie Down in Darkness." *Commonweal*, 55 (19 October 1951), pp. 43-44.

Prescott, Orville. "Book of the Times." *New York Times*, 10 September 1951, p. 19.

Rubin,Louis D., Jr. "What to Do About Chaos." *Hopkins* Review, 5 (Fall 1951), pp. 65-68.

Scott, J. D. "New Novels. *New Statesman and Nation*, 43 (19 April 1952), pp. 472-73.

Swados Harvey. "First Novel." *Nation*, 272 (24 November 1951), pp. 453.

"The Unbeautiful and Damned." *Time*, 58 (10 September 1951), pp. 106, 108.

Set This House on Fire:

Adams, Phoebe. *Atlantic Monthly*. 206 (July 1960), pp. 97-98.

Baro, Gene. "Styron's New Novel: Search for the Meaning of Evil." *New York Herald Tribune Book Review*, 5 June 1960, pp. 1, 12.

Borklund, Elmer. "Fiction of Violence and Pain." *Commentary* 30 (November 1960), pp. 452-54.

Breit, Harvey. "A Second Novel." *Partisan Review*, (Summer 1960), pp. 561-63.

Curley, Thomas F. "The Quarrel with Time in American Fiction." *American Scholar*, 29 (Autumn 1960), pp. 552-60.

Dahms, Joseph G. *America*, 103 (18 June 1960), pp. 380-81.

Fenton, Charles A. "William Styron and the Age of the Slob." *South Atlantic Quarterly*, 59 (Autumn 1960), pp. 469-476.

Fuller, Edmund. "A Picture of Hell by a Writer of Maturing Vision." *Chicago Sunday Tribune Magazine of Books*, 5 June 1960, p. 3.

Hicks, Granville. "After the Fury, a Time of Peace." *Saturday Review of Literature*, 43 (4 June 1960), p. 13.

Highet, Gilbert. *Book-of-the-Month-Club News*, June 1960, p. 7.

Hollander, John. *Yale Review*, 50 (Fall 1960), pp. 152-53.

Hutchens, John K. *New York Herald Tribune*, 3 June 1960, p. 11.

"Just Out: A Kind of Tenderness. *Newsweek*, 55 (6 June 1960), pp. 117-18.

Kirsch, Robert R. "Styron's 'House' Nears Greatness." *Los Angeles Times*, 5 June 1960, p. 7-C.

Kohn, Sherwood. "Styron . . . an heir of Camus ?" *Louisville* (Ky.) *Times*, 15 June 1960, p. 11.

Lea, George. " New Novel Won't Set House on Fire." *Chicago Sun-Times*, 10 July 1960, sec. 3, p. 5.

Miller, Nolan. *Antioch Review*, 20 (Summer 1960), p. 256.

Mizener, Arthur. "Some People of Our Time." *New York Times Book Review*, 5 June 1950, pp. 3, 26.

Monaghan, Charles. "Styronic Manner." *Commonweal*, 72 (22 July 1960), p. 380.

Newberry Mike. "Shock of Recognition." *Mainstream*, 13 (September 1960), pp. 61-63.

New Mexico Quarterly, 30 (Winter 1960-61), p. 412.

Pickrel, Paul. "Heroic Proportions." *Harper's*, 221 (July 1960), p. 93.

Prescott, Orville. *New York Times*, 3 June 1960, p. 29.

Price, Emerson. "Magnificent Novel Portrays Man Trapped by His Own Folly." *Cleveland Press*, 7 June 1960, p. 28.

Rothberg, Abraham. "Styron's Appointment in Sambuco." *New Leader*, 43 (4-11 July 1960), pp. 24-27.

Rubin, Louis D., Jr. "An Artist in Bonds." *Sewanee Review*, 69 (Winter 1961), pp. 174-79.

———. *Baltimore Evening Sun*, 3 June 1960, p. 30.

Scott, Paul. *New Statesman and Nation*, 61 (17 February 1961), pp. 270-71.

Sherman, John K. "Melodrama of Good and Evil Probes Human Undercurrents." *Minneapolis Tribune*, 12 June 1960, p. 6-E.

Southern, Terry. *Nation*, 192 (19 November 1960), p. 382.

Virginia Quarterly Review, 36 (Autumn 1960), p. civ.

"What Happened at Sambuco." *London Times Literary Supplement*, 17 February 1961, p. 101.

The Confessions of Nat Turner:

Bryden, Ronald. Slave Rising. *New Statesman*, 75 (3 May 1968), pp. 586-87.

Buckmaster, Henrietta. "Racism, 1831: The Fire Last Time." *Christian Science Monitor*, 12 October 1967, p. 5.

Coles, Robert. "Blacklash." *Partisan Review*, 35 (Winter 1968), pp. 128-33.

Collier, Peter. "Saga of Rebellion." *Progressive*, December 1967, pp. 41-42.

"Confessions of Nat Turner Condemned as Racist Book." *Los Angeles Free Press*, 29 March 1968, p. 8.

Cooke, Michael. "Nat Turner's Revolt." *Yale Review*, 57 (Winter 1968), pp. 273-78.

Core, George. "*Nat Turner* and the Final Reckoning of Things *Southern Review*, n. s. 4 (July 1968), pp. 745-51.

Delany, Lloyd Tom. "A Psychologist Looks at *The Confessions of Nat Turner*," *Psychology Today*, 1 (January 1968), pp. 11-14.

Duberman, Martin. *Village Voice*, 14 December 1967, pp. 8-9, 16.

Fremont-Smith, Eliot. "A Sword Is Sharpened." *New York Times*. 3 October 1967, p. 45.

———."The Confessions of Nat Turner'—II." *New York Times*. 4 October 1967, p. 45.

Friedman, Melvin J. "*The Confessions of Nat Turner*: The Convergence of 'Non-fiction Novel' and 'Meditation on History." *Journal of Popular Culture*, 1 (Fall 1967), pp.166-75. See also *The University of Wisconsin at Milwaukee Magazine*, Spring 1968, pp. 3-7 (abridged).

Fuller, Edmund. "Power and Eloquence in New Styron Novel". *Wall Street Journal*, 4 October 1967, p. 16.

Gilman, Richard. "Nat Turner Revisited." *New Republic*, 158 (27 April 1968), pp. 23-26, 28, 32.

Goodheart, Eugene. "When Slaves Revolt." *Midstream*, 14 (January 1968), pp. 69-72.

Harnack, Curtis. "The Quidities of Detail." *Kenyon Review*, 30 (Winter 1968), pp. 125-32.

Hicks, Granville. "Race Riot, 1831." *Saturday Review*, 50 (7 October 1967), pp. 29-31.

———. "Five for Year's End." *Saturday Review*, 50 (30 December 1967), p. 19.

Hogan, William. "William Styron's American Tragedy." *San Francisco Chronicle*, 9 October 1967, p. 43.

———. "Further Thoughts on the Styron Novel." *San Francisco Chronicle*, 10 October 1967, p. 39.

"The Idea of Hope." *Time*, 90 (13 October 1967), pp. 110, 113.

Kauffman, Stanley. "Styron's Unwritten Novel." *Hudson Review*, 20 (Winter 1967-68), pp. 675-79.

Kazin, Alfred. "Instinct for Tragedy: A Message in Black and White." *Book World*, 8 October 1967, pp. 1, 22.

Lehan, Richard. *Contemporary Literature*, 9 (Autumn 1968), pp. 540-42.

McGroaty, Rev. Joseph G. " 'Nat Turner': A Racial Tract for Our Times." *Tablet*, 60 (16 November 1967), p. 13.

McPherson, James Lowell. America's Slave Revolt." *Dissent*, 15 (January-February 1968), pp. 86-89.

Mason, Robert. "A Brilliant 'Meditation on History'—Nat Turner, from Birth to Rebellion." *Virginia Pilot and Portsmouth Star*, 8 October 1967, p. 6-C.

Meyer, June. "Spokesmen for the Blacks." *Nation* 205 (4 December 1967), p. 597.

Miller, William Lee. "The Meditations of William Styron." *Reporter*, 37 (16 November 1967), pp. 42-46.

Murray, Albert. "A Troublesome Property." *New Leader*, 10 (4 December 1967), pp. 18-20.

Nolte, William H. "Fact Novel of Revolt in Hot Summer of 1831." *St. Louis Sunday Post-Dispatch*, 8 October 1967, p. 4-D.

Platt, Gerald M. "A Sociologist Looks at *The Confessions of Nat Turner*." *Psychology Today*, 1(January 1968), pp. 14-15.

Rahv, Phillip, "Through the Midst of Jerusalem." *New York Review of Books*, 9 (26 October 1967), pp. 6, 8, 10.

Richter, David H. *Chicago Literary Review*, October 1967, pp. 1, 10-11.

Rubin, Louis D., Jr, "Books—Eloquent Story of a Slave Rebellion." *Washington (D.C.) Sunday Star*, 8 October 1967, p. 14-D.

———. "William Styron and Human Bondage: *The Confessions of Nat Turner*." *Hollins Critic*, 4 (December 1967), pp. 1-12.

Sheed, Wilfrid. "The Slave Who Became a Man." *New York Times Book Review*, 8 October 1967, pp. 1-3, 30, 32, 34.

Sokolov, Raymond A. "Into the Mind of Nat Turner." *Newsweek*, 70 (16 October 1967), pp. 65-69.

Steiner, George. "Books—The Fire Last Time." *New Yorker*, 43 (25 November 1967), p. 236.

Thompson, John. "Rise and Slay !" *Commentary*,, 44 (November 1967), pp. 81-85.

Tucker, Martin. *Commonweal*, 87 (22 December 1967), pp. 338-39.

"Unslavish Fidelity: The Confessions of William Styron." *London Times Literary Supplement*, 9 May 1968, p. 480.

Virginia Quarterly Review, 44 (Winter 1968), p. viii.

Weber, R.W. "Styron's Power Creates a Real Being." *Louisville (Ky.) Times*, 13 October 1967, p. 11-A.

Woodward, C. Vann. "Confessions of a Rebel: 1831. "New *Republic*, 15 (7 October 1967), pp. 25-28.

In the Clap Shack:

Brockway, Jody. *Theatre Crafts*, 6 (June 1973), p. 44.

Leon, Phillip W. "Styron Publishes First Play." *Nashville Tennesseean*, 2 September 1973, p. 10-E.

Publishers Weekly, 203 (7 May 1973), p. 63.

Spearman, William. Chapel Hill (N.C.) *Weekly*, 8 July 1973, p. 4-C.

Washington (D.C) Post, 15 July 1973, *Book World*, p. 15.

E. *Violence, Compassion. The South and Tragic Humanism*:

Backman, Melvin. *Faulkner: The Major Years A Critical Study*. Bloomington and London: Indiana Univ. Press, 1966.

Barrett, William. *Irrational Man: A Study in Existential Philosophy*. New York: Doubleday, 1958.

Bergonzi, Bernard. *The Situation of the Novel* (Penguin Books). Harmondsworth: Penguin, 1972.

Bewkes, Eugene C., et al. *The Western Heritage of Faith and Reason.* New York: Harper and Row, 1963.

Blackham, H.J. *Six Existentialist Thinkers.* New York: Harper, and Brothers, 1959.

Bowra, C.M. *Ancient Greek Literature.* London: Oxford University Press, 1967.

———. *The Romantic Imagination.* London: Oxford University Press, 1973.

Bree, Germaine. *Camus: A Collection of Critical Essays.* Twentieth Century Views. Englewood Cliffs, N.J.: Prentice-Hall, 1962.

Bronowski, Jacob. *The Face of Violence: An Essay with a Play.* Cleveland: World, 1967.

Camus, Albert. *The Rebel.* London: Hamish Hamilton, 1960.

———. *The Myth of Sisyphus.* Harmondsworth: Penguin, 1975. (Justin O'Brien, translator)

Camus, Albert. *The Plague.* London: Hutchinson Educational, 1967. (Stuart Gilbert translator)

Cash, W.J. *The Mind of the South.* New York: Vintage Book, 1941.

Chander, Jagdish, ed. *Perspectives in American Literature,* Ludhiana: Lyall Book Depot, 1969.

Clayton, John J. *Saul Bellow: In Defence of Man.* New Delhi: Allied, 1970. First Indian Edition.

Cohen, Hennig, ed. *The American Culture: Approaches to the Study of the United States.* Hyderabad: American Studies Research Centre, 1972.

Cowan, Michael H. *Twentieth Century Interpretations of the Sound and the Fury: A Collection of Critical Essays,* Engelwood Cliffs, N.J.: Prentice-Hall, 1968.

Ellmann, Richard: Charles Feidelson, Jr. *The Modern Tradition Backgrounds of Modern Literature.* New York: Oxford Univ. Press, 1966.

Faulkner, Peter. *Modernism.* London: Methuen, 1977.

Fitzgerald, Sally and Robert Fitzgerald, eds. *Mystery and Manners*. New York: Noonday, 1970.

Foerster, Norman, ed. *American Poetry and Prose*. Boston: Houghton Miffiin Company, 1962. 4th ed. Part II.

Ford, Boris, ed. *The Modern Age*. London: Cassell, 1966.

Frohock, Wilbur Merrill. *The Novel of Violence in America*. Dallas: Southern Methodist University Press, 1958.

Fromm, Erich. *The Anatomy of Human Destructiveness*. New York: Holt, 1973.

———. *The Heart of Man, Its Genius for Good and Evil*. New York: Harper, 1964.

———. *Man for Himself: An Enquiry into the Psychology of Ethics*. New York: Holt, 1947.

Fuller, Edmund. *Man in Modern Fiction: Some Minority Opinions on Contemporary American Writing*. New York: Random House, 1958.

George, A.C. *T.S. Eliot: His Mind and Art*. Bombay: Asia Publishing House, 1962.

Harper, Howard M., Jr. *Desperate Faith: A Study of Bellow, Salinger, Mailer, Baldwin and Updike*. Chapel Hill: University of North Carolina Press, 1967.

Hoffman, Frederick J. and Olga. Vickery, eds. *William Faulkner: Three Decades of Criticism*. New York and Burlingame: Harcourt, Brace and World, 1963.

Horton, Rod W. and Herbert W. Edwards. *Backgrounds of American Literary Thought*. Englewood Cliffs, N.J.: Prentice-Hall, 1974.

Howe, Irving. *William Faulkner: A Critical Study*. Chicago and London: The Univ. of Chicago Press, 1975.

Johnson, Pamela Hansford, *The Art of Thomas Wolfe*, New York: Charles Scribner's Sons, 1963.

Kern, Edith. *Sartre: A Collection of Critical Essays* (Twentieth Century Views) Englewood Cliffs, N.J.: Prentice-Hall, 1962.

Kierkegaard, Soren. *The Sickness Unto Death*. Princeton, N.J.: Princeton University Press, 1941. (Trans. Walter Lowrie)

Krieger, Murray. *The Tragic Vision.* Chicago and London: The University of Chicago Press, 1966.

Leifer, Walter ed. *Man and Modern Time.* Munchen: Max Hueber, 1962.

Lewis, R.W.B. *Trials of the World.* New Haven and London: Yale University Press, 1966.

———. *The Picaresque Saint: Representative Figures in Contemporary Fiction.* New York, Philadelphia: Lippincott Company, 1959.

Litz, A. Walton. *Modern American Fiction: Essays in Criticism.* New York: Oxford Univ. Press, 1967.

Lukacs, George. *The Historical Novel.* Boston: Beacon Press, 1963. (Translated from German by Hannah and Stanley Mitchell)

May, Rollo. *Power and Innocence: A Search for the Sources of Violence.* New York: W.W. Norton, 1972.

Miller, Arthur. *Arthur Miller's Collected Plays.* New Delhi: Allied, 1973.

Milligate, Michael. *Faulkner.* Edinburgh and London: Oliver and Boyd, 1966.

Perkins, George. *The Theory of the American Novel.* New York: Holt, Rinehart and Winston, 1970.

Richter, David H. *Fable's End: Completeness and Closure in Rhetorical Fiction.* Chicago and London: The University of Chicago Press, 1974.

Rubin, Louis D., Jr. and Robert D. Jacobs., eds. *South: Modern Southern Literature in its Cultural Setting.* Carbondale: Southern Illinois University Press, 1966.

——. *William Elliot's Shoots a Bear: Essays on the Southern Literary Imagination.* Baton Rouge; Louisiana State University Press, 1975.

Sartre, J.P. *Existentialism* and *Humanism.* London: Eyre Methuen, 1973. (Trans. Philip Mairet)

Satyanarayana, M.R. *John Steinbeck: A Study in the Theme of Compassion*, Hyderabad, 1977.

Schiller, F.C.S. *Studies in Humanism.* Westport, Conn. Greenwood Press, 1970.

Sewall, Richard. *The Vision of Tragedy.* New Haven and London: Yale University Press, 1970.

Scott, Nathon A., Jr., ed. *The Climate of Faith in Modern Literature.* New York: The Seabury Press, 1964.

Spiller, R.E. et. al., ed. *Literary History of the United States: History.* New Delhi: Amerind Publishing Co., 1963.

Thomas, J. Heywood, Jr. *Subjectivity and Paradox: A Study of Kierkegaard.* Oxford: Basil Blackwell, 1957.

Thompson, Lawrence, *William Faulkner: An Introduction and Interpretation.* New York: Holti Rinehart and Winston, 1967.

Thorp, Willard. *American Writing in the Twentieth Century.* Cambridge, Mass.: Harvard University Press, 1963.

Tillich, Paul. *Christianity and the Encounter of the World Religions.* New York: Columbia University Press, 1963.

Toynbee, Arnold. *Christianity Among the Religions of the World.* London: Oxford Univ. Press, 1968.

Vinson, James, ed. *Contemporary Novelists.* London: St. James Press, 1972.

Volpe, Edmund L. *A Reader's Guide to William Faulkner.* London: Thames and Hudson, 1964.

Waldmeir, Joseph J., ed. *Recent American Fiction: Some Critical Views.* Boston: Hougthon Miffiin Company, 1963.

Warren, Robert Penn, ed. *Faulkner.* Twentieth Century Views: Englewood Cliffs, N.J.: Prentice-Hall, 1966.

West, Paul, *The Modern Novel,* Volume 2. London: Hutchinson University Library, 1967.

INDEX